Who by Plague

High Holy Days Sermons from COVID19 Times

Edited by Rabbi Dr. Oren Z. Steinitz

Forward by Rabbi Joshua Lesser

Cover Design: Yael Steinitz

ISBN: 9798714886805

Imprint: Independently published by Hamotzi Press
http://www.hamotzipress.com

Table of Contents

FORWARD
DREAMING UPSIDE DOWN

Rabbi Joshua Lesser

It was Purim and I had a funny feeling. It was not a "haha" kind of funny. No, actually, *v'nahafoch hu*[1], quite *the opposite had occurred*. Little did I know that that we were about to experience an *olam hafuch*[2], a world turned on its head. And in retrospect, 2020 was about to give us a crash course on the mystical teaching that *Yom Kippurim* was actually *Yom K'Purim* (Yom Kippurim is a day like Purim) and its reverse: that Purim also shared much in common with Yom Kippur. Everything was about to be turned upside down.

The morning of *Erev Purim,* I left a voicemail for a congregant who was a public health worker, asking about how worried I should be about this emerging virus and the synagogue. However, when it went to voicemail, I let my preoccupations with Purim takeover. Wanting to shake up Purim, and host a meaningful and joyful experience, I decided to change up the format.

What if, post-Megillah reading, instead of acting out the less than perfect *shpiel* we decided upon, what if Purim was to be a true celebration of unmasking our talents and unmuting our authentic self-expression. Could Purim be a vehicle to support people revealing their hidden talents? Thus, the "Oh-So-Gay-Purim-Cabaret!" was born.

---

[1] Esther 9:1
[2] Pesachim 50a

We rented out a coffee shop that was set up with a stage and lights to host musical performances. Not only did we recruit congregants with diverse talents like singing, parodies, stand up comedy, story telling, poetry reading and clowning, but we received a small grant to pair them with coaches to support their talents.

It far exceeded my expectations. Little did we know that the phrase "social distancing" was about to be coined, but we were packed like sardines in this coffee shop, singing, acting and laughing our hearts out, all using the same two microphones! The unity and pride could have been measured by the enthusiastic aerosols dancing around us, if I would have had the notion to think that way. Our last time together was one part sophisticated fun, one part raucous speakeasy and one part Jewish communal soul--and stir! If we were to watch a playback of this, knowing what we know now, we would likely feel as if we were watching a horror movie, knowingly yelling at the screen, "No, don't do it!"

One of the connections between Purim and Yom Kippur is the idea that the collective people's fate is tied to a lottery. Both accounts, whether it was the date of the destruction of the Jewish people by Haman or the fate of the goats, symbolizing the seeming randomness of who will live and who will die. Both of these have the power to render us helpless, seeking compassion and choosing how we might live with active hope. These feelings that were discovered on or before Purim as the pandemic emerged, became even more intensified on a Yom Kippur that was radically transformed. For me, the two will forever be linked.

I have always preferred Yom Kippur to Purim. I can far more easily access solemnity and a desire for self improvement than I can sheer unmitigated playful fun. Too often, it feels forced; but that Purim was sublime. I have returned to that near-perfect Purim in my head, because the day after Purim my phone rang and my heart stopped. Trying to understand all of the details, I was urged by the many public health care workers to start making arrangements to prepare the congregation for a pandemic. The Corona Virus was here. To underscore the point, the emcee of our Purim cabaret had flu-like systems, which required an immediate letter to the congregation.

Rabbi Joseph B. Soloveitchik taught that "Perhaps the feature common to both Purim and Yom Kippur is that aspect of Purim which is a call for Divine compassion and intercession, a mood of petition arising out of great distress." Out of my own distress, I knew it was time to do a *Heshbon HaNefesh*. "How would I navigate this in a spiritually aligned way?" I wondered.

At first I felt guilt. Should I have been paying closer attention? I have learned that in moments when I am overwhelmed, I need some mindful spaciousness, despite the urgency. In my own contemplative *tefilah*, I recognized that the weight of this and all of the impending decisions and consequences was too much to bear alone. I also knew that not every congregation had the blessing of having dozens of public health workers as I do. A crazy thought emerged, "What if I convened a group of one hundred or so of my closest colleagues to brainstorm, share resources and offer emotional support to one another?" My first impulse was to make this a multifaith Facebook group for spiritual leaders. The day after Purim, March 11th 2020, the Spiritual and Communal Responses to Covid-19: A Resource for Clergy and Spiritual Leaders.

Days later, people were joining by the hundreds. Dozens of posts a day asked for support and resources. Zoom, to most of us, was the noise a car made. We balanced the need to transform our congregations onto virtual platforms, offer pastoral care, tend to the sick, officiate funerals, navigate new restrictions, process the unfolding discoveries and address our own life challenges. The incredible compassion, resourcefulness and resilience was a brilliant outpouring. Without the benefit of an Adar Bet, the rabbis and cantors started swapping ideas regarding how to lead Pesach in this upside down world and then it hit us.

By the time Passover arrived, the news that this pandemic would not be over by summer was just being assimilated. Combatting the dread and resistance were Rabbi Michael Latz and others who understood that High Holy Days would need to reenvisioned. Using the group that I founded, he called together colleagues and hosted a Zoom meeting to discuss how might we approach High Holy Days. As a result of that meeting, we understood that this was not an undertaking that one Zoom call could achieve and so I created a second group called "Dreaming Up High Holy Days".

And dream, we did. Once again, the world upended, *olam hafuch,* but in an incredibly positive way. This time, in the face of being dealt a pandemic in Life's lottery, we chose to make Yom Kippur more like Purim. In the face of our collective survival – as institutions, as communities, as a people, we sought to increase joy by expanding Jewish creativity, and solidarity. Like Purim, when our future is at stake we were willing to take risks and try new things, and like Yom Kippur, we understood that our wellbeing is not just individual but collective.

Therefore, we convened a group of moderators with different expertise (including the editor of this collection) and together we put hundreds of hours into fostering a community that chose not to abide by business as usual. Instead, we sought to break down turf, exclusivity and competition. With no grant money and no institutional barriers to navigate, our only incentive was our sheer commitment to the common good and a desire to serve Jewish peoplehood well. Jewish leaders from all movements joined together to keep this virtual world spinning and from this dream emerged our High Holy Day reality. From this reality, sprang this collection of sermons and *drashot*.

This collection is nothing short of a symbol of the breathtaking resilience of our community. The diversity of voices and perspectives speak to the extraordinary ways that we can put our primary differences aside for the benefit of *klal yisrael,* the entirety of the Jewish people. Just like Purim centers the margins, I would be remiss in pointing out that a majority of us who supported this container represent an aspect of the margins of Jewish community. Just as the psalmist reflects that it is the Jewish way to overturn, "the stone that was put aside has become the cornerstone." When understanding the container with the exceptional messages that came from such a fraught, yet important time in the Jewish people's collective experience, one should finish this assembly of voices with the profound understanding that it is the myriad of our voices that best reflect God's presence in the world, and the willingness that speaks of Jewish leadership at its most generous.

Many of our communities experienced an unprecedented connection and joy despite the losses that we incurred during the pandemic. While many of us would have chosen to be physically present, the intention poured into these days broke virtual boundaries. The Vilna Gaon comments that there are two exceptions to the Talmudic description that holy days are half for the Divine and half for humanity: Yom Kippur and Purim. Yom Kippur is all spiritual and Purim is all embodied. Yom Kippur invites us to reflect on life's fragility in the face of our mortality; whereas Purim suggests that we cultivate joy and pleasure in light of it. Yet in this past pandemic year, my Purim inspired a greater sense of soul searching, of mortality and the dangers of its denial; whereas, my Yom Kippur and the entirety of the Days of Awe brought me great pleasure in the davening and celebrating a resilient connected people. Most of us lived the teaching in an unimaginable visceral way, that Purim and Yom Kippur are two halves of the same whole.

This linkage from Purim to Yom Kippur helped so many communities transcend surviving the High Holy Days and transform them into experiences that helped people thrive in the face of suffering. In many ways, the Facebook Group *Dreaming Up High Holy Days* served as both a physical support and a spiritual inspiration. These powerful teachings are also inextricably linked, because none of them would have truly existed without the care, instruction and sharing of the community which we are a part of. Knowing that all of these sermons are deeply connected should remind us that we can experience both a Purim-like joy and a Yom Kippur yearning even in the face of a pandemic, great losses and the sacred Days of Awe. Perhaps it is this combination and wondrous mutual care that is the secret to winning the Lottery of Life.

This introductory essay is dedicated to the moderators who joined me in incredible stewardship of Dreaming Up High Holy Days, not Dreaming Up 5781 (listed alphabetically backwards because after all, the world is upside down): Cantor Cheryl Wunch, Rabbi Oren Steinitz, Leo Mindel, Rabbi Michael Adam Latz, Rabbi Stephanie Kolin, and Rabbi Shira Koch Epstein.

Rabbi Joshua Lesser *has proudly served as the Senior Rabbi at a progressive and creative synagogue Congregation Bet Haverim for 22 years and will soon become Emeritus. He trained as a spiritual director with Lev Shomeia and has been a director for nearly a decade. He has also led spiritual direction groups for people exploring grief, for activists and advocates and for those exploring the spirituality of creativity. He currently serves on the Mayor of Atlanta's LGBTQ Taskforce board and is the recent Past Chair of the City of Atlanta's Human Relations Commission. Rabbi Lesser is the rabbinic editor of Torah Queeries, a Weekly Bible Commentary and the founder of the Southern Jewish Resources Network for Gender and Sexual Diversity. The founder of the Facebook groups, Spiritual and Communal Responses to Covid-19 and Dreaming Up 5781, he has been dedicated to ways that clergy and spiritual leaders might best support each other during the pandemic.*

JUDAISM'S MOST BASIC QUESTIONS

Rabbi Rachel Ain

The High Holidays are upon us. On one hand, it has felt like the longest year ever and yet, I can't believe it's already September. What am I supposed to say to you, this morning? What could you possibly need to hear? Preparing for these high holidays has been one of the hardest so far in my career. Not because there aren't plenty of ideas to reflect on, but because, of the enormity of the shift in our landscape this year. **Of course,** it created a sense of awe, but we are still living through it, so quite frankly it is hard to find ways to tie it all up in 5 sermons.

But I will try. I will try to get at the essence of what it means to be Jewish overall, what Judaism says to us in these trying times, and how we can use the tools, techniques, and history of being Jewish to give us the strength to contemplate life's most important questions. I will NOT be doing all of that this morning :)

This morning, I want to reflect on the lessons we might learn from 2020, specifically through the lens of COVID-19 and what our Jewish tradition can teach us as we understand what are our most basic needs. And so my job is not to tell you the news that you can easily access on the many different stations that it appears, but I hope that this morning, I can use this time to share how I think the wisdom of Judaism can help frame this moment because I believe that **that** is a role of a synagogue. To help you see how Judaism can be a lens through which you can articulate and process your everyday desires, thoughts, and experiences.

Let me begin personally.

This has been a scary time which is a fitting way to start a RH sermon, because our Torah readings evoke fear. Sarah's fear of the loss of the love of her husband, Hagar and Ishmael's fear of hunger and homelessness, Isaac's fear of loss of life and I could only assume Abraham's fear of being responsible for all of this pain. I imagine that all of us have weathered these emotions to different degrees. The fear of not knowing what the next day will be like. I remember in early April, I couldn't sleep. I had a cough that wouldn't go away and I was taking my temperature every few hours. While I didn't have covid-19, I felt that the invisible tidal wave of the disease was just a few feet away and that it could, at any moment, overtake us. Let me be clear. I know that people had it much worse than me-people lost loved ones, people were sick, people are sick. But the fear that so many of us felt in March, April, and May in particular, when we were just trying to flatten the curve, caused me to have many sleepless nights.

So I stayed up late into the evening and began writing down those values that are important to me, so that, in the scary event that in a blink of an eye I wouldn't be able to communicate, my family would know what was important to me.

"It is April 2, 2020 and I am writing these thoughts, as I stay up, each night, not being able to fall asleep. I am so scared. I am scared that since I have been sick since

February, something might happen to me. I am scared for Dave. I am scared for my kids. On one hand, I am very proud of my life. I have a wonderful husband, great kids, a successful career, great friends, and feel bound to a wonderful community. But I don't want to die. I don't want to say goodbye yet to my kids. They still have so much growing to do and I want to be here to see that.

On that late night in April, I continued to write: "There is so much pain and disaster right now. People are going to starve. We have a full pantry of food and a refrigerator that I keep restocking. Ok, it doesn't have exactly what I might want in a given moment but it has more than most and for that, I am grateful." Of course, as you can see, I was ok. I was just "regular" sick...but the emotions I felt were strong, even though I was ok.

But I wasn't only scared for myself. I was scared for our community. I was scared for many of you. Those who are older. Those who are sick. Those who work in hospitals. I was scared that you didn't have what you need and that we wouldn't know. I was scared that I would fail you, and if I did, I am sorry. I hope you will forgive me.

And so I continued to ask myself questions that to me, help us frame how to enter this new year, so i share some of these questions with you that I have used when teaching about ethical wills.

If you knew that you were potentially going to face death (as we all do) to whom would you address your thoughts at this moment?

For me, it is certainly to my children, Jared and Zack. As of the writing Jared was 14 and Zack was almost 12. Jared was in 9th grade at Heschel and Zack was in 6th grade at Schechter Manhattan. I am so proud of them. They are kind, sensitive, and yet normal teens! They both have their moments where they can drive each other or me nutty but the love that they have for each other and for us as parents is something that makes me smile.

WHO WOULD YOU SPEAK TO?

Another question: What were formative events in your life? For me, it was A) Going to camp Ramah as a child and then again as a counselor B) Switching to JDS in 8th grade D) Going on Poland/Pilgrimage and deciding to become Kosher E) Going to Ramah in the summer of 1994 which led me to Barnard F) The tree incident of 1995 at camp which made me think about God on a daily basis G) Meeting Dave freshman year at Simchat Torah at Erica Newman's house-his influence on me to join the DD program; his willingness to marry and celebrate a woman who wanted to be rabbi :) H) Buying tefillin from my rabbi, Rabbi Cahan I) Being hugely disappointed by my other childhood rabbi J) My summer serving as a navy chaplain cadet K) Living in Israel during The 2nd intifada L) The death of three young people within 15 months when I was a rabbi in Syracuse M) The birth of my children N) Challenging and successful job searches. S) The loss of my grandparents Q) And so much more... What were moments that were formative in your life?

Who influenced you the most? There is no question that there are people that I can point to-people who had an impact on me as a child until today and people I have known more than half my life. My parents and grandparents have and had attributes of a strong work ethic, a commitment to the Jewish community, a love of their children and extended family, an understanding that learning is a lifelong endeavor, the importance of generosity, and so much more. They all, in their own ways showed me how to be a better person, professional, community leader, and caregiver. I am forever indebted to what I have learned and what I continue to learn from them.

My sister Dorie, who I am grateful is part of my life, not just as family but as my closest, go to friend. I have learned from Dorie that you need to share your feelings out loud, that you should be expressive in all parts of your life, and you should enjoy documenting every moment.

When I was 18 years old, I met two people, Dave, and his mom Ellen, who also have influenced me greatly. They have taught me how to make every moment an experience, every item a precious treasure, every birthday and hallmark holiday one to celebrate, and that no obstacles are out of reach. I learned perseverance and strength through them.

And: What are some of the important lessons that you learned in life?

A) It is really important to work hard-and while some people (like me) start with a huge leg up, privilege because of what my parents had accomplished and could provide for me as a child and a young person, it is also hard work and work ethic make a difference in how you perceive of yourself and how others perceive you. But i also know that sometimes, even with hard work there are times that we encounter many roadblocks, and we need to move the roadblocks for ourselves and others when we see them unfairly placed int the road.

B) Don't expect life to be fair even if you have done everything right (accidents happen). Bad things occur.

C) Our heart can expand, it doesn't get divided into smaller pieces when you meet more people to love. Loving someone else does not diminish one's love for someone already there.

D) Things can't be neatly tied up in a bow, as much as you might want them to-life is messy. I try to live in the center. Extremism is bad even if it feels easier to market. In fact, last year, my sermon was about balance! But being a passionate centrist is how I have lived my life and how I encourage others to do so and that brings me to the question of why ask these questions if we are all going to have different answers?

The reason is, we need to understand what is at stake. Each of us matters. Each of us has wisdom to share. But we also need to find wisdom in our tradition to help frame our experiences right now for the big questions and the questions that enable us to go through each day.

On Rosh Hashanah we have an opportunity to reflect on that which is important to us and we have a chance to reset-so what can we learn? How do we evaluate the past several months through the lens of our Jewish tradition?

First, we recognize that though there are moments that we all feel that we are in the dark, we know that the sun will emerge-and so we need to look to our tradition for hope and perspective and sometimes for a reminder of what is important.

So here are the Jewish lessons that all of us can learn from COVID as we enter into this new year regardless of how we answered the first sets of questions:

First, as *Pirke Avot* asks, who is wise? One who learns from all – It means that I don't know everything and I shouldn't believe someone who feels that they know everything. Rather, we should know what we know and know what we don't know. It means having people to go to, to ask questions. It is why, as your religious leader, I believe I have a religious obligation to keep everyone safe and it is why we have taken a conservative approach to this year's holidays. And it means that I need to ask questions, for the times that we are in person, and so: what does it mean to learn from everyone? It means that I have been able to lean on the doctors and other experts in our midst to ask important questions for all of our health and safety and for that, i am grateful.

The next question that I believed emerged for all of us, during these days, is also from *Pirke Avot*:

Pirke Avot asks: who is rich? And the rabbis answer their own question by saying: The one who is satisfied with their lot. Money didn't define satisfaction this spring, toilet paper and Clorox wipes did. Being able to have essential items-the basics-cleaning supplies, food, masks, that is what the essential items are. Even today it is almost impossible to find Clorox wipes! Yes, we want more than that. Of course. So did I. But we began to focus on what essential means. And of course, we started using that word for people-who are essential people? Who are essential workers? What are essential businesses? That is clear-the doctors, nurses, scientists, grocery store workers, public transportation drivers, EMTS and Police who transported people to hospitals, those in maintenance at the hospitals, nursing homes, those in the military, and teachers, and more, who couldn't work virtually. They showed up, each and every day, putting themselves (and often their families) at risk because they didn't pay attention to their own individual needs, but understood that they were a part of a collective. It is why we applauded them each night, ritually, as a token of our support. To all of you at home, who helped this world on our behalf, I thank you for the bottom of my heart and my soul. You are essential. You are needed. And we will all be forever grateful. And to all of us that stayed home, thank you. Our staying home enabled essential workers to do what they needed to do.

COVID taught us that we live the phrase: *Al Tifrosh Min HaTzibur.* **Do not separate from the community. Now you might find it ironic that I am using that phrase as we are all sitting separate from one another. But the fact is, what we learned this year is that just because we might be physically distanced, doesn't mean we can't and shouldn't be spiritually connected.**

It means that *Kol Yisrael Arevim Zeh BaZeh*, all of Israel is responsible for one another is a phrase that we must live out. We must support each other, our community, our institutions. We need to realize that in order to be together next year, we need to be together this year. So thank you, for committed to the SPS community.

Marcelo Gleiser, the 2019 Templeton Prize Laureate, and the Appleton Professor of Natural Philosophy at Dartmouth College, wrote:

> COVID-19 will change us as a species. We must respond not just as nations fighting an enemy, but as a species fighting for survival. The virus will not wipe us out. But it is causing untold pain and loss, destabilizing global markets, and turning our daily lives into a surreal dreamscape. Our vulnerability and co-dependence are openly exposed.
>
> Nature doesn't care about our arrogance. A tiny organism is forcing us to revisit our values, our divisions, our choices as we barricade within our homes with our closest family members and consider what will come next. We can taste the anxiety in our mouths, imagining what will happen if we lose internet connectivity, or run out of food and resources or worse, contract the virus.
>
> We would be foolish not to embrace the central message of our predicament: that we must come together to survive....

We must think collectively as a human hive, each of us playing an essential role. The first steps are simple: to be humble in the face of what we don't know, to be respectful of nature and its powers, and to work together to preserve not just our lives and those of our loved ones, but the lives of all of us in the hive, young and old, celebrating the gift of being alive."

The gift of being alive. Yes, for sure. At this moment, we can and must celebrate the gift of being alive.

That despite our fear we can find resilience in appreciating that which is essential

That despite our loneliness we can find community around us, even virtually.

That despite our disappointment, we can find silver linings.

I often share at baby namings the Hasidic teaching that "when there is a birth of a new baby, the world begins anew." I truly believe that we are in the midst of watching a new world emerging. I am hoping that it is one of appreciating all those who are essential. Finding the capacity to be grateful for what we have. And opting into community as opposed to opting out.

Here at SPS we are cultivating opportunities to help with this-to think deeply about the essential values and ideas of Judaism and Jewish community. We know that we need to look deeply at what is important. And we will. This hasn't been an easy year. I know that so many people wish that this time, 2020, could just be canceled and we could have a do-over.

Leslie Dwight wrote:

>What if 2020 isn't cancelled?
>
>What if 2020 is the year we've been waiting for?
>
>A year so uncomfortable, so painful, so scary, so raw — that it finally forces us to grow.
>
>A year that screams so loud, finally awakening us from our ignorant slumber.
>
>A year we finally accept the need for change.
>
>Declare change. Work for change. Become the change. A year we finally band together, instead of pushing each other further apart.
>
>2020 isn't cancelled, but rather the most important year of them all.

As we turn the corner into 5781 let us do it with the presence of mind and the tenacity of spirit that we aren't going anywhere, rather, we are asking ourselves important questions, we are learning from this year, and we are forging ahead to live the values and the history that makes us who we truly want to be.

Shana Tova.

Rabbi Rachel Ain *is the rabbi at Sutton Place Synagogue in Midtown Manhattan. She sits on the Chancellor's Rabbinic Cabinet of JTS, is a co-chair of the Rabbinic Roundtable at the American Jewish Committee and on the Executive Board of the NY Board of Rabbis. She has studied at the Shalom Hartman Institute in Jerusalem. During Rabbinical School she served as a commissioned Lieutenant (JG) for the US Navy Chaplains Corps. In 2018 She was awarded the Tikun Olam award by the Jewish Council on Public Affairs. She was ordained by JTS in 2004 and is married to Rabbi David Levy, the Director of the Ramah Sports Academy. They are the proud parents of two sons.*

ON THE NECESSITY OF FALLING APART

Elliott batTzedek

This has been a year.

This has been about ten years.

One's impulse on Yom Kippur is always to look back, to reflect on "this time last year."

Honestly, can any of you remember what your most pressing worry was this time last year?

That, I suppose, is a lesson in the power of perspective.

Ever since COVID closed down our lives, I've read so many wise essays on how to keep perspective, how to avoid depression, how to stave off loneliness, how to keep positive, how to put on your jester hat and smile and pretend you can go on keeping all your balls in the air.

What I'm here to share now is none of that advice. I'm here to share the opposite of that advice. I'm here to tell you to fall apart.

Or at least to say this: it's okay to fall apart.

No one can or should be holding it together all day every day in these times. Our forests are on fire, our ice sheets are melting, we're in the middle of the first of what are bound to be many new viruses to come, and there's a very real and urgent threat that corporate fascists are going to take total control over our country.

And that's my view on a good day. No wonder that, some days, I just can't hold it together and need to lock the door, cry, let myself feel terrified and hopeless, let myself feel the immensity of these problems, let myself know that we are beyond any ability to "go back to normal" and our best hope is that human creativity and generosity will somehow become bigger than greed and the powerful turn-on of power over.

I'm here not just to tell you that it's okay to fall apart, but that you really ought to be falling apart, sometimes, if you're not yet doing that. Because if you're not yet falling apart, sometimes, you're running your body and mind on the non-stop cortisol of fight-or-flight, and that this will burn you out, burn you up, consume your resources for bouncing back when you do crash. I know – I was one of those kids whose flight-mechanism was always on, so I lived flooded with cortisol, and, believe me, there are so many better ways to live. Far better that you fall apart, sometimes, that you give in and acknowledge that the pressures of this world are more than anyone can handle. Your long-term survival may well depend not on how well you stay positive, but on how successfully you are able to fall apart completely, sometimes.

Contemporary studies about stress and trauma and mental health certainly say this – and so does our own tradition, in its way. The rabbis of the Jerusalem Talmud understood the model of private prayer to be Hannah, sob-praying on the steps of the Temple because she could not conceive a child. There the High Priest, Eli, assumed she was drunk because she had so completely fallen apart. Being that broken-hearted, that shattered, and so that vulnerable was, the sages announced, THE model that all petitioners to god should follow. Prayer SHOULD come only when we have fallen apart completely – being all positive and peppy and resilient is the language of memes, not the language of prayer.

Of course, the sages who used Hannah's honest, fragile grief as the model of all prayer also completely excluded their own peers – actual living women they knew - from the core of Jewish religious practice and meaning-making. I, being an actual living woman, can't focus on their teaching without also focusing on how they thought of me as less than fully human. If you feel the urge to recommend to me that I find a way to be more positive about this, perhaps you should revisit my third sentence back.

But I chose to become a Jew, as a feminist, not because I didn't know what the sages thought of me, but because I can only survive if I fall apart, sometimes, and Judaism not only knows this, but honors it. Not only honors it, but has only grown and evolved because of having fallen apart. The Torah as we know it began in the terror of having lost everything after the burning and looting of the First Temple. Rabbinic Judaism came about when the Jewish world fell apart after the destruction of the Second Temple – when there was no "normal" to go back to, creating something new and moving forward was the only option. Knowing how to completely fall apart, sometimes, is encoded in our High Holy Days. Hannah's story is right here, the official Haftorah on Rosh Hashanah (even if we usually do other liturgy). The heart of Rosh Hoshanah is the shofar service – a service I've sounded now for 15 or so years. The muscles and cells of my lips, my face, my chest, my hands – all resonate throughout the year from the cry of the shofar. And that sound is a cry – not just a crying out, but an actual sobbing. The shofar service is designed such that the sound completely falls apart into shattered pieces. There are years, this one in particular, where I felt like I should have just finished it there, refused to blow the final long note, because doing so promises some kind of healing, of redemption, and September 2020 is definitely not a time of redemption.

Which means, while I finished the shofar service last week with a call of redemption, I can't honor the call to fall apart, sometimes, with any kind of happy or uplifting resolution with my words today. The instinct to tell one another "buck up" or "it will get better" or "you'll bounce back" is the exact opposite of being present to one another is the midst of moments of unresolvable pain. What I want to honor is the moment of falling apart, and the courage to sit in witness as others fall apart. So I close with this – when you are falling apart – and you need to, sometimes – know that I see you. I will sit with you and, unlike the High Priest, not report you to the authorities for being drunk. I will never, ever, call you crazy, or less than, or broken, because needing to break, sometimes, is how we will survive together.

In the words of poet/translator/liturgist Marcia Falk:

ON THE NECESSITY OF FALLING APART

It is ours to praise
the beauty of the world
even as we discern
the torn world.

For nothing is whole
that is not first rent

Elliott batTzedek, MFA, *is a poet, liturgist, translator, and bookseller. She lives in Philadelphia, where she has been co-leading Fringes: a feminist, non-Zionist Havurah since 2007. Her liturgies for shabbat and holidays have been used across the U.S. Her translations of the Israeli lesbian poet Shez won the Robert Bly translation award and are forthcoming.*

WHO AM I, THAT I SHOULD CONFRONT PHARAOH?

Rabbi Adam Chalom

If you were Moses, what would you do? You see a bush on fire that is not consumed. A voice calls you by name, claiming to be the god of your ancestors. It has heard the suffering of Hebrew slavery, and it promises to deliver them to a land flowing with milk and honey. Then the voice says, "I will send you to Pharaoh to bring out my people, the children of Israel, from Egypt." What would you do? This is no hallucination. You did not choose this situation; until recently you had a comfortable life, an adopted son of Egyptian royalty. You fled Egypt after killing an overseer who was beating a Hebrew slave. And now you must go back to the scene of your crime, address your people's suffering, challenge power face to face. What does Moses do? He asks a question. "Who am I, that I should confront Pharaoh?"

A simple yet profound question: who am I? It is simple because early in life, we learn to respond to the sound of our own names. Even coma patients can show brain activity when they hear their names. "Who am I" is profound because if you do not know who you are, how can you know others? How can you experience the world if not from the fixed point of the self? This question can be an escape, hiding behind the anonymity of just a normal person – "Who am I" meaning I am nobody, and a nobody does nothing. This question can also be a challenge – who am I really, am I the person I want to be? "Who am I" can be an out or a commitment.

Which would you have chosen as Moses? Which do you choose today?

Being Jewish is our particular subset of the human experience. Some Jewish questions are Jewish specific – which *haroset* recipe for Passover do you like the best? What lessons do you draw from Jewish history? Other Jewish questions speak to the human condition. The very act of asking questions is both very Jewish and very human – I believe every language has words for "why" and "how." The universal human quest for "why" and "how" is the basis of science, history, knowledge based on evidence. Jews do not have a monopoly on asking questions, just like we do not have a monopoly on guilt – ask any ex-Catholic. Yet asking questions can STILL be very Jewish – a key element of the Passover seder is the four questions. One way that modern Jews differ from our forebearers is that we are more open to new answers, even heretical answers, even to challenging the questions themselves. To be fair, though, one of Moses' defining characteristics is his chutzpah [nerve]. When Noah is told to build the ark and save only his family, he asks no questions. When Moses is commanded, he asks many questions, starting with "Why me?"

More precisely, "Who am I that I should confront Pharaoh?" Perhaps Moses suspects there will be more to do than just snap his fingers to free the Israelites. Spoiler alert: Moses' work will not be over from now until the end of the Torah – after the burning bush there will be 40 more years of leading, negotiating and arguing to get this stubborn, stiff-necked people to the Promised Land.

19

In our own days, you do not need me to tell you that WE face many challenges. We face them as Americans, as the Jewish family, as human beings. The Passover Haggadah describes 10 plagues that Moses inflicts on Pharaoh and the Egyptians; 2020 has 10 plagues beaten easily. In no particular order:

Racism, sexism, homophobia, hyper-partisanship, rising temperatures and extreme weather, policing and the criminal justice system, poverty and hunger, domestic violence, constitutional crisis du jour, massive budget and pension shortfalls, health care, automation and job disruption, government corruption, cyberprivacy and the pitfalls of social media, immigration policy, hurricanes and killer wasps. And, of course, the plague of coronavirus which includes illness, death, shutdowns, school openings, school closings, economic disruption, videoconference overload… and a Rosh Hashana when we are together emotionally but the sanctuary is empty.

Facing all of our plagues, our Pharaohs, we also ask, "Why me? Who am I to confront all of this, and how much longer?" The challenges are overwhelming, and we have no confidence in a guaranteed happy ending. In the real world, there IS no promised land flowing with milk and honey, no pillar of cloud by day and fire by night to show us where to go. Yet the people we deal with are just as stubborn and stiff-necked as ever!

And we are not Moses. Of course, at the start of his saga even Moses was not Moses. He was uncertain, asking for help, avoiding responsibility. A leader after 40 years had better be different than a leader in year one. Preparing for a funeral for a woman who died in her 90s, I first met with her children, who were seniors themselves. They had had a challenging relationship with her as a mother when they were small children. I also talked separately with her grandchildren, who had experienced her very differently – she had been loving, generous, caring and interested in their lives. Those who are grandparents know that parenting and grandparenting are very different. The experience is also different because the adult is different – this grandmother was 30 years older and wiser with different responsibilities from when she was a mother to small children. Everyone has had experiences we look back on and say, "If only I'd handled that differently." We cannot expect to have lived our lives then with what we know now. Part of letting go of misdeeds and omissions at the Jewish New Year, our own or those of others, is to not expect anyone to have been perfect from the beginning.

It does not matter that we are not yet Moses; we will probably never be Moses. A Hasidic story told by Martin Buber makes the point: Rabbi Zusya once said, "In the coming world they will not ask me: 'Zusya, why were you not Moses?' Instead, they will ask me: 'Why were you not Zusya?'" We do not have to be Moses, and we do not have to solve every problem I listed to make a difference. We do have to be our version of Zusya – our best self. And we do have to act, because not acting is also a choice, no matter who you are.

Yes, the Pharaohs we face are daunting. Some "Pharaohs" are systemic from a nation's founding, be it race in America or Arabs in a self-defined Jewish state and its territories. Some are the result of generations of bad decisions and short-sighted leadership unable to make hard choices. Some are unforeseen consequences of good intentions. Some are the result of cruelty, indifference, or a lack of empathy.

For the moment, though, imagine you are at a summer camp, standing at the deep end of the pool in the morning. You know the water will be cold when you jump in. You know you get better every time you swim, and once you start swimming the water will not feel as cold. Going in one toe at a time will be just as cold and take much longer to get through. The hardest part is making that decision to take the leap. We can certainly get more information before we act – dip a toe in the water, ask a friend who has already jumped. Moses himself asks many questions.

Here's the dialogue, image it in instant message format:

> "Go free the Israelites from Pharaoh."
> "Who am I to go to Pharaoh to free the Israelites?"
> "Don't worry, I will be with you."
> "The Israelites will ask me later, so tell me now: who are YOU to send me?" (in other words, "who dis?")
> "Tell them I am the god of their fathers and they will listen."
> "What if they don't believe me and think I imagined all this?"
> "Here are some signs and wonders – make your staff into a snake and back,

turn your hand leprous and then heal it.
If those don't work, we'll turn the Nile
to blood."
"I am slow of speech and slow of
tongue, please send someone else."

You get the sense that Moses really does NOT want the job.

We could make our own excuses to avoid acting – I did not create the problem, even if I benefit from it. I am not trying to hurt anyone. These problems are beyond my ability to solve. Why should people listen to me, I'm no Moses; I'm not even a Zusya. And I do not even know enough to know where to begin, even if I decide to act. These excuses may all be true. But they not good enough to do nothing. We can all move the ball forward, even if only a little. In Pirke Avot [Sayings of the Ancestors] 2:15, Rabbi Tarfon said, "the day is short, and the work is plentiful . . . . It is not your duty to finish the work, but neither are you free to neglect it." Our day is still short, there is still plenty of work, and we cannot rely on others to get it done.

Sometimes if you want something done right, or done at all, you have to start it yourself.

"Who am I, that I should confront Pharaoh?" We reject this question as escape – we may not finish the work, but we are not free to neglect it. Instead it is a commitment: what do we each have in our personal toolbox to bring to bear to the problems we face? It may be more than we realize.

Some of us have financial resources. The need for tzedakah or righteous giving is deep for many worthy causes, and there are people doing good work consistent with any political or religious ideology. But generosity is not a function of raw dollars. Did you know that those who earn less money often give a higher percentage of their income in charitable donations? In 2016, among those who itemized, those earning $50,000 to $100,000 donated 1% MORE of their adjusted gross income than those earning $500,000 to $2 million. The higher earners gave more dollars but were less generous. Amazon tycoon Jeff Bezos has a net worth around $200 billion. If he donated $20 million, that would be same as someone worth $200,000 donating $20. Do not ask why you cannot be Bill Gates – look at who you are and go from there.

Some of us have educational resources. We are good at reading or writing or explaining. We can deepen our understanding of the challenges: their origins, their persistence, their possible solutions. We can motivate others to change behavior and work for the good. We can connect with family or friends who might listen to us when they do not listen to strangers. Moses' first worry is not whether Yahweh will convince Pharaoh to free the Israelites – Moses doubts the ISRAELITES will believe it can happen, so he must convince them first! If change starts at home, we can start by connecting with those we know best.

Some of us have privilege. You can be privileged in some ways and disadvantaged in others. Ashkenazi Jews are not white to Nazi white nationalists, but they may be treated as white by loan officers or police officers. I am definitely white if I go to the beach without sunblock! Acknowledging privilege does not mean apologizing for something you did not do or being shamed for who you are. This is not the oppression Olympics where the most suffering wins. If you do have inherited wealth, or visually white skin, or standard English, you start the race of life some steps ahead of those without those advantages.

We sometimes hear an absolute choice: either equality of opportunity or equality of result. Either everyone has an unweighted fair opportunity to succeed on merit alone, or equal end results are imposed through boosting some and weighing down others. In the real world, we all get to that starting line from different beginnings, through different experiences, with different assets. If certain names or accents or skin colors are less likely to get a good education or housing or equal treatment by the justice system, then we need to pay special attention to what happens before the starting line in order to have real equality of opportunity.

What do we do if we are on the more fortunate side of perceived race and education and income? We use it to do good. Moses was an Israelite adopted by Pharaoh's daughter. He did not have to intervene to save the Hebrew being beaten by the Egyptian taskmaster, long before he heard the voice. After the killing, Moses had escaped, far away from Egypt. He went back to Egypt to help others. So, too, did the 19th century "Moses," Harriet Tubman, who escaped from slavery in 1849 only to return 13 times to rescue at least 70 fellow slaves. She did not free herself and then leave others to do the same;

she went back at great risk to herself to help show them the way.

All of us have opportunities. We do not have to wait for a burning bush or a voice from the heavens to act. We no longer need freedom riders on interstate busses, but freedom walkers, freedom voters, freedom citizens can still make a difference. To make that difference, we have to accept the challenge of "who am I" – what are my values, and how valuable are my values to my sense of self?

When Moses meets the burning bush, it is an external authority, a god who tells him what he must do. Even if Moses asks some questions, he knows and the readers know who is really in charge. Our task today is more challenging. If we ask "who am I, that I should confront today's Pharaohs," we do not expect an answer from beyond. The answer must come from within.

You do not have to be a prophet, a Moses, a god. You are Zusya; you are Harriet; you are YOU. You are the only you there is, and if you do not bring who you are and what you have to push for the changes you want to see, then you will have missed this unique opportunity, a moment that will never come again.

In Pirke Avot 4:13, we read, "There are three crowns – the crown of Torah, the crown of the priesthood, and the crown of royalty; but the crown of a good name is greater than all of them." What makes your name great? You do. So make your name great by what you do with who you are. Call received. Answer awaited.

Rabbi Adam Chalom *serves Kol Hadash Humanistic Congregation in suburban Chicago. He is also Dean for North America of the International Institute for Secular Humanistic Judaism (IISHJ), on the Executive Committee of the Association of Humanistic Rabbis, and on the Editorial Board of Humanistic Judaism magazine. Rabbi Chalom holds a BA in Judaic Studies from Yale University, rabbinic ordination from the IISHJ and a Ph.D. in Near Eastern Studies from the University of Michigan. He lives in Highland Park, Illinois with his wife and two children.*

SHELTER OF RELATIONSHIPS

Rabbi Margaret Frisch Klein

Today I want to talk about a tough topic. The Shelter of Relationships. Today's Torah portion, like yesterday's is amongst the most difficult in scripture. Abraham hears a voice telling him to take his son, his only son, the one he loves, Isaac and offer him as a sacrifice. His response, "Hineini. Here am I. I'm ready." Unlike when G-d tells him that G-d is about to destroy Sodom and Gemorah, he doesn't ask a question. He doesn't challenge G-d. He doesn't ask his partner, his co-parent, Sarah. He goes. He is ready.

There is lots that could be said about this text. A whole book, *But Where is the Lamb*, explores all of the midrashim from three different religious traditions.

However, I want to talk about what happens after. It seems he pushed Ishmael away—we read that text yesterday. And Isaac seems to live, although some of the midrashim have a different outcome. What happens after that? The text is not clear. Did Abraham and Isaac both return to Beer Sheva?

What we do know is that after this story is over, Sarah dies. And the years of her life were one hundred and twenty and seven. Abraham comes to mourn her. To bury her. In Kiryat Arba. Wait, what? There seems to be a gap in the text. He comes to bury her? In Kiryat Arba? Wasn't he in Beer Sheva? How did she get to Kiryat Arba?. Sarah seems to have died alone.

Abraham buys a burial plot. Apparently, he eulogizes her. The midrash tells us that the eulogy was what we call "A Woman of Valor" from the Book of Proverbs Chapter 31. In traditional Jewish families this is read to the woman of the house every Friday night. *Eishet Chayil.*

> A Woman of Valor,
> who can find for her price is far above rubies.
> The heart of her husband safely trusts in her,
> And he has no lack of gain.
> She does him good and not evil
> all the days of her life.
> She seeks wool and flax,
> And works willingly with her hands.
> She is like the merchant-s hips;
> She brings her food from afar.
> She rises also while it is yet night,
> And gives food to her household,
> And a portion to her maidens.
> She considers a field, and buys it;
> With the fruit of her hands she plants a
> vineyard.
> She girds her loins with strength,
> And makes strong her arms.
> She perceives that her merchandise is good;
> Her lamp goes not out by night.
> She lays her hands to the distaff,
> And her hands hold the spindle.
> She stretches out her hand to the poor;
> Yea, she reaches forth her hands to the needy.
> She is not afraid of the snow for her
> household;

For all her household are clothed with scarlet.
She makes for herself coverlets;
Her clothing is fine linen and purple.
Her husband is known in the gates,
When he sits among the elders of the land.
She makes linen garments and sells them;
And delivers girdles unto the merchant.
Strength and dignity are her clothing;
And she laughs at the time to come.
She opens her mouth with wisdom;
And the law of kindness is on her tongue.
She looks well to the ways of her household,
And eats not the bread of idleness.
Her children rise up, and call her blessed;
Her husband also, and he praises her:
'Many daughters have done valiantly,
But you rise above them all.'
Grace is deceitful, and beauty is vain;
But a woman that fears the LORD,
she shall be praised.
Give her of the fruit of her hands;
And let her works praise her in the gates.

It is a lovely reading. One I used to argue with my own mother about. She did not think it was a feminist enough text for her. We did not use it at her funeral. In our house we use it as a checklist. Yes, I rose before dawn. Yes, I wasn't idle. Yes, I fed the hungry and my staff. Yes, I have purple clothes. No. still not opening my mouth with wisdom and the law of kindness is still not on my tongue often enough. I am not alone in that. Many of the "sins" that we will confess next week have to do with speech. About 65% of them.

The law of kindness is on her tongue. This is a year where we will need that. For all of us.

We need kindness in our speech. We need kindness with ourselves. We need to show acts of kindness as our Talmud text tells us to bury the dead and console the bereaved. Burying the dead is actually an act of *chesed shel emet*, lovingkindness of truth, because this is the last act that you will do for someone and you cannot expect to be paid back for it.

So Abraham uses this checklist, this eulogy to describe Sarah. And to this day, we use this reading at funerals for women.

Fast forward. Abraham dies. He also seems to die alone. Isaac and Ishmael come back together to bury their father. But only after their father dies. Some years I see their coming back together as a sign of hope. If Isaac and Ishmael can do it, can Israelis and Palestinians? This year, in a year when so many have died alone, without the comfort of a loving family member near by, I find it sad that both Sarah and Abraham seem to have died alone.

Perhaps the message in yesterday's text and today's text is this. Don't assume you know what G-d wants. G-d does not want you to sacrifice your children. G-d does not want you to be alone. G-d wants you to reconcile, to bridge the gap. To take the first step if necessary.

The earlier part of Genesis tells us that G-d created men and women equal. That G-d did not want Adam to be alone. That he needed a helpmate. Rosh Hashanah and

Yom Kippur beg us. It is not too late. Now is the time. Don't be like Abraham. Don't push your children away. Repair your relationships. And if you can't, then mourn the relationship you wish you could have had. The time is now.

This has been a year when have seen the images of too many people dying alone. Not by their choice and not by the choice of their families but because of this global pandemic. In actuality they were not alone. They were often surrounded by Superheroes—those caring and compassionate caregivers, doctors and nurses and support staff who helped families dial in, who held hands, who administered care and even, in some cases, prayed. And G-d was with them.

Rabbi Margaret Wenig is a great story teller and a professor of homiletics at Hebrew Union College. She writes personally and speaks almost whimsically. One Rosh Hashanah she told the story of G-d being an aging woman, looking through the Book of Memories, we might call it the Book of Life. The end of her sermon,

"God holds our face in her two hands and whispers, "Do not be afraid, I will be faithful to the promise I made to you when you were young. I will be with you. Even to your old age I will be with you. When you are grey headed still I will hold you. I gave birth to you, I carried you. I will hold you still. Grow old along with me...."

Our fear of the future is tempered now by curiosity. The universe is infinite. Unlimited possibilities are arrayed before us still. We can awaken each morning to wonder:

What shall I learn today? What can I create today? What will I notice that I have never seen before?

It has been a good visit. Before we leave, it is our turn to take a good look at God. The face which time has marked looks not frail to us now—but wise. For we understand that God knows those things only the passage of time can teach: that one can survive the loss of a love; that one can feel secure even in the midst of an ever changing world; that there is dignity in being alive even when every bone aches. God's movements seem not slow to us—but strong and intent, unlike our own. For we are too busy to see beneath the surface. We speak too rapidly to truly listen, and we move too quickly to feel what we touch. We form opinions too fast to judge honestly. While God, God moves slowly and with intention. God sees everything there is to see, understands everything God hears, and touches all that lives.

Ahh, that is why we were created to grow older: each added day of life, each new year make us more like God who is ever growing older.

How often do we sit in the house of prayer holding in our hands pages of greeting cards bound together into a prayer book, hundreds of words we ourselves have not written. Will we merely place our signatures at the bottom and drop the cards – the prayer book – in the mail?

God would prefer that we come home. She is waiting for us, ever patiently until we are ready. God will not sleep.

She will leave the door open and the candles burning waiting patiently for us to come home.

Perhaps one day...perhaps one day we will be able to look into God's aging face and say, "Avinu Malkeinu, our Parent, our Ruler, we have come home."

This story reminded me of the novel the Shack that was then made into a movie. It is really a midrash on how we imagine G-d. But G-d takes us in and loves us and heals us.

Mackenzie Allen Phillips's youngest daughter, Missy, was kidnapped and murdered during a family vacation in Oregon. Four years later, in the midst of his Great Sadness, Mack receives a suspicious note, apparently from God, inviting him back to that shack for a weekend. Against his better judgment he arrives at the shack on a wintry afternoon and walks back into his darkest nightmare. What he find there will change his life forever. The book forces us to confront some of our deepest questions. It makes us wrestle with G-d. Where is G-d in a world so filled with unspeakable pain? How can we be in relationship with others, or with G-d.

G-d was there. G-d is there. G-d will be there. However, we imagine G-d. For all of us who struggle with relationships, who feel we may alone. We are not. G-d is with us. As I have sung in far too many hospital rooms the end of Adon Olam says:

> Into your hands I commit my spirit, my
> soul. You neither slumber or sleep. G-d is
> with me. I shall not fear.

34

May it be so for each of us. That we know, in our deepest, inner selves that we are never alone and thus we have no fear.

This morning, early, before dawn I was called to the hospital. It was my first hospital visit in 8 months. I didn't hesitate. I went. I pulled into the hospital's ER parking lot. I was met by a young CPE student who quickly signed me in and ushered me into the ICU. "You must be someone really important." No, just someone who could sing this very song. Some one who could offer a few words of comfort. Someone who could cry.

Rabbi Margaret Frisch Klein *is the rabbi of Congregation Kneseth Israel in Elgin, IL. She blogs as the Energizer Rabbi, www.theenergizerrabbi.org and has written two books, one on the 13 Attributes of the Divine, Climbing Toward Yom Kippur and the other on Enduring Spirit on healing from domestic abuse and sexual assault using the cycle of the Jewish year. She has several additional poem/prayers published. She was ordained from the Academy for Jewish Religion in New York and serves as the secretary of the Association of Rabbis and Cantors. She finds great spirituality in the rhythm of running.*

EMBRACING SELF-COMPASSION ON YOM HADIN (THE DAY OF JUDGMENT)

Rabbi Lauren Grabelle Herrmann

I want to start this morning with some truth telling:

In the past year:

-I let my kids watch TV or play video games for hours—no, days—on end

-I ignored my work at moments where my kids needed me

-I ignored my kids at moments at moments when they needed me

-I did not reach out to friends for help, support, or companionship nearly as much as I needed

-I yelled at or picked fights with my partner at a significantly higher frequency, and I stayed mad longer.

-I did not engage in nearly as much self-care as my body and soul craved.

Lest you think I have forgotten that it is Rosh HaShanah and not Yom Kippur, I share these things not because I am confessing my sins to you. Rather, I share them to name some of the things I am offering myself compassion for over these Days of Awe.

Today is *Yom HaDin*: the Day of Judgment. According to the Mishnah (the first Jewish law code), all of humanity passes before the Holy One for judgment on Rosh HaShanah (*Mishnah Rosh HaShanah* 1:2). As we say, in the *Unetane Tokef*: On Rosh HaShanah the decree is written, on Yom Kippur it is sealed.

Even if we do not subscribe to a theology that includes Divine Judgment, the theme remains central to our contemporary holiday observance. We engage in *Cheshbon HaNefesh*, an accounting of our soul and actions. And as the inauguration of the *aseret y'mei teshuvah*, the ten days of turning/repentance, Rosh HaShanah invites a critical eye and self-judgment, as we consider the ways in which we have missed the mark and how we can do better in the coming year.

Yet, according to Jewish tradition, Rosh HaShanah is in its essence a day of *rachamim*, compassion. A midrash (rabbinic teaching) teaches: "On Rosh HaShanah, When the Holy Blessed One ascends to sit on the throne of judgment on Rosh Hashanah, God ascends for judgment. Once the people of Israel take their *shofarot* and blow them, what does the Holy Blessed One do? God rises from the throne of judgement and sits on the throne of compassion, and is filled with compassion for the people and transforms the quality of justice into the quality of compassion." (Vayikra Rabbah 29:3)

As modern Jews, we may not believe that God literally sits on a throne of judgment. Yet we look to the texts of our tradition as a mirror and instructions for our lives. This text teaches us what our seat or vantage point should be on *Yom HaDin*.

Self-judgment may be necessary, but it is neither helpful or productive to dwell there forever, to criticize or beat ourselves up. Bringing compassion to our imperfect and painful places, our mistakes and wrongdoings, is equally and perhaps even more important. And as the midrash states- it is our actions that determine this shift: the power to choose between judgment and compassion is in our hands.

While self-compassion is important on any Rosh HaShanah, it feels critical to our mental and spiritual health as we enter this new year, 5781. We are in the middle of a global pandemic. Our lives have been upended and disrupted. Some of us more than others for sure, but even still, all of us in some way. Our relationships have been strained, either because we are not able to see people we love at all or with regularity or because we are seeing the people we care about with too much frequency!

The pandemic is a set up for failure, because we cannot do the things we normally do that make us feel productive and because we are on edge and exhausted. And we are living through unprecedented, anxiety-provoking times as we watch the manifestations of climate change, worry about the future of our country — which just became even more heightened in the last twenty four hours with the tragic loss of Ruth Bader Ginsburg. We feel concern over growing anti-Semitism, and see, and for some experience first-hand, the horrors of racism. Meanwhile, each of us carries the individual burdens we bear under the best of times. How could anyone be their best selves under these circumstances?

38

In times such as these, moving from self-judgment to self-compassion isn't just a good idea, it is a spiritual necessity. It is what will help us meet this moment and even thrive under these difficult circumstances.

We don't become masters of self-compassion overnight. Like anything else that is meaningful, we have to work at it and build our self-compassion muscles. To that end, today, I will speak about two principles, rooted in Jewish texts, to help us grow our self-compassion. The first is "letting go of perfectionism" and the second is "loving ourselves as we love our neighbors."

Letting go of perfectionism.

I recently learned a beautiful teaching from my colleague Rabbi Stephanie Kolin. A midrash tells that when Moses was to construct the *mikdash*, the tabernacle, he felt insecure and asked God: How can I possibly construct this Tabernacle, knowing that I am only human and cannot make it perfect like you or your ministering angels?

And God returned: I have celestial materials above. You do not need to use my materials, you have your materials down below; if you build the *mishkan* with the materials you have, in your earthly plane, I will come and dwell there. (Bamidbar Rabbah 12:8)

This fictional conversation between God and Moses offers a remarkable teaching for all of us, especially those of us who bend toward perfectionism: Do not judge yourself by a godly standard, something

39

unattainable to reach. Use what you have: your talents, your resources. Perfection is not only impossible, it is not desired. What you create and what you build will be not only good enough; it will be holy.

This is Torah that speaks right to my soul, as I lean toward perfectionism in almost every area of my life. And while perfectionism can sometimes help me write that great sermon or push me to take on new projects, it also has a shadow side that often stops me from feeling joy or satisfaction.

The pandemic has really challenged this perfectionism for me, especially in the area of parenting. In a flash, I was not just a mom and a rabbi. I was a mom, a rabbi, a teacher, a supervisor, a playmate, a chef, and a personal secretary all at the same time. I felt like I was failing all the time. In March and April, I felt terrible about the amount of screen-time that my kids were enjoying, my lack of presence, and basically: all of it.

In May, my husband Jon shared something he read in a Times article about parenting during the pandemic. A mom in Fremont, California, said: "Our goal is to survive: no divorce, no getting fired and no children running away from home. If we can do that, I will consider us a success story."

Without exaggeration, this perspective has saved me. Now, whenever I start complaining about how bad a job I am doing at this pandemic parenting thing or when I see my kids are behaving in ways I normally would feel terrible about, I repeat to myself- or have Jon repeat to me- that mantra: "No divorce, no getting fired, and no running away from home." That is success.

As we learned in the midrash, we are not to judge ourselves by godly standards. Perfection is not desired. We build with what we have.

Loving Ourselves as We Love Our Neighbors

There is a debate in the Talmud about what is the most important verse in the torah. Ben Azzai cites a verse about the generations of Adam, bringing us back to our central humanity. Rabbi Avika asserts: "*V'ahavta l'reacha kamocha*": Love your neighbor as yourself.

On this debate, Rabbi Brad Artson says, "We are all supposed to think that Rabbi Akiva is right … (as he is the Torah scholar par excellence).[3] But I want to say that he got it backwards. The challenge, I think, is not loving our fellows the way we love ourselves. We are all pretty good at giving people the benefit of the doubt. I think the challenge is loving ourselves in the way we have been trained to respond to other people's pain."

It is important to note that the Hebrew object is "*re'acha*" -not the stranger, not the countryman, but the neighbor. Someone you are in a relationship with, who knows our spouse or children if you have them, someone in our community, a person you trust and have affection for.

Let's play this out for a moment. If you have a neighbor or friend who is going through a difficult time, what

---

[3] https://ikar-la.org/sermons/the-gift-of-self-compassion-rabbi-dr-bradley-shavit-artson/

would you do? You would listen to them, offer sympathy. If that friend was expressing impatience at not being in the place that she wanted to be in her physical or spiritual life, you would refrain from judging their progress, instead urging them to be patient and that everything would be ok. If you had a friend going through a hard time, you would likely make them casserole or two or organize a meal train!

Let's take Rabbi Artson's challenge, flipping the order of the phrase: to love ourselves as we love our neighbors. When we are having a difficult moment, do we offer ourselves sympathy/empathy? Do we refrain from judgment and offer reassurance? Are we willing to ask for the help and support that we need — perhaps in the form of meals, rides, walks, company? For most of us, our answer is no or not really. But that's the work.

Anne Lamott, author and spiritual teacher, writes about mercy, which she defines as "radical kindness."[4] She says, "Probably the most radical part of it all is that it begins with kindness to yourself in the same measure with which you would be very, very kind to others. Sort of automatically — [we] are warm and friendly to other people…. And yet with ourselves, we tend to be harsh. And we tend to be easily exasperated with ourselves. So, the radical part of kindness is about stroking your own shoulder and stopping the bad self-talk. And that's where my belief in healing — both ourselves and our families and the world — begins, is that we put our own oxygen masks on first."

---

[4] https://www.dinnerpartydownload.org/anne-lamott/

Some may say that given all we are facing in the world, self-compassion is a luxury. I am convinced that it is essential. When we are depleted and struggling, self-compassion brings us back to life: to the moment, not some fantasy of what should be happening, but what's happening right now. And self-compassion is a gateway to laughter, to acceptance, and to joy — all of which fuels our work in the world.

Whatever we build in the coming year, whatever we create or manage and whatever we face, I want to invite us to hold onto that image of Moses building the Tabernacle and know that we just need to give our best effort with the materials we have been given and it will be exactly as it should be. Whatever we are struggling with or holding, let us offer the kind of kindness and generosity we would with our neighbors and friends.

May this *Yom HaDin*, Day of Judgment, be sweetened with *Rachamim*, compassion. May we remember that the power to choose between harsh self-scrutiny and self-compassion is always in our hands.

Shana Tova.

Rabbi Lauren Grabelle Herrmann *is the rabbi of SAJ-Judaism that Stands for All, the first Reconstructionist synagogue in America. Rabbi Lauren's rabbiniate at SAJ and formerly at Kol Tzedek Synagogue which she founded is focused on bringing people and voices from the margins into the center and on integrating Jewish spirituality and the work of social justice. She is a member of T'ruah and New Sanctuary Coalition and co-chair of the Rabbinic Council of Jews for Racial and Economic Justice.*

LOVE

Rabbi Lisa Gelber

Rabbi Moshe Leib of Sassov, 18thc. disciple of the Maggid Mezritch overhears two people in conversation. One says to the other, *I love you.* The other objects saying, *If you really love me, tell me what's hurting me.* Rabbi Moshe Leib goes on to teach, *This is a profound lesson. No one really loves a neighbor until we know what causes them pain.* The intensity of an emotion such as love calls us to connect with something under the surface, in the depths of our being. To love a neighbor requires us to open to the messy, to embrace not just joy and friendship but to know complexity and pain. How well do we really know one another? How well do we even know ourselves? Take a moment. Ask yourself. What is hurting me? What are you carrying that alters sensations in your body, causes distress, anguish or annoyance. What aches within? These are not easy questions. The ache of one does not match the ache of another. We can't always know the pain of another. Peloton instructor Tunde Oyeneyin talks about a paper cut in her Speak Up ride. How can you know the pain of a tiny paper cut until you've experienced it? Who would fathom the thinnest separation of skin could cause searing pain? The deepest pains of life do not heal so easily as a paper cut.

This morning, we read of Abraham responding to Gd's call to offer up his favorite son as sacrifice. *Vayashkem Avraham baboker*/Early the next morning Abraham gets his things together and takes his servant and his son Isaac to go to the place Gd told him about (Gen 22:3).

Avraham gets up early to take his son - *et y'hidkha asher ahavta et Yitzhak*/the favored one, whom he loves, Yitzhak. *Asher ahavta*. Whom you love. Gd tells Abraham to sacrifice his son, whom he LOVES. Dear Gd. I wonder. Does Avraham know what causes his son pain? Dear Gd. Do you know what causes Avraham pain? You know the man must feel pain. He might get up early to do your bidding, but he walks for three days with his head down. *Bayom hashishi vayisa Avraham et ainav vayar et hamakom mayrahok*/on the third day Abraham looked up and saw the place from far away (Gen. 22:4). Having put the wood for the offering on his son Isaac, taken the firestone and the knife, Abraham walks off with his son. Isaac says to his father, A*bba. Avi. Where is the sheep for the offering* (Gen 22:7)? Dear Gd. Avraham must know what causes his son pain. *Avraham responds, Gd will see to the sheep for this offering b'nee. My son, the Holy One will attend to this* (Gen 22:8). Thank Gd. You must know what causes Avraham pain. Perhaps that is why Avraham does not speak as he does with Sodom and G'morrah. Perhaps that is why he cannot bear to look up for three whole days. We find it easy to judge Avraham for responding to Gd's call. Do we know what pains him? Do we know his inner conflict, his struggle?

Carol Gilligan talks about what it means to engage in radical listening and see the world from another's perspective, raising the question of how to have empathy for people from whom you are afraid. For a long time, I was afraid of Avraham. What kind of leader does this, sacrificing his child (not really in the end), sacrificing himself for a growing ideology that does not see beyond that system of ideas and ideals? It has taken years of immersion and questioning and reflecting and struggling with this text for me to imagine Avraham's pain and feel a sense of empathy. Micha Goodman, research fellow at the Shalom Hartman Institute in Jerusalem maintains that paying attention is a precondition for empathy. Looking beyond oneself. Using our senses to notice, listen and see what another is experiencing. Perhaps it is only when we can truly empathize that we know what causes another pain.

Torah teaches, *Love your neighbor as yourself/v'ahavta l'reyacha k'mocha* (Lev.19:18). Not so easy or clear as we might think. Many are taught to put themselves first. Put your neighbor first just as you put yourself first? Are you really the same? How does one do that? Others are taught to put others before themselves, always. That might be good for your neighbor but what does that mean for you? How does one then come to know, appreciate and honor oneself? I think we need to start from the self. Know what it means to bear the weight of pain. Pay attention to how you move in the world. **Do not take the invitation to love for granted**. Remember that we are given love because we have *n'shama eloheet*/a holy and gdly soul. This connects our essence and the essence of another. We are bound to connect with others. The Torah presupposes that we will be in relationship, the question is how.

Thornton Wilder writes, *There is a land of the living and a land of the dead and the bridge is love, the only survival, the only meaning* (The Bridge of San Luis Rey). We have spent much of this year living between the land of the living and the land of the dead, literally and figuratively. We've had close to 250 thousand cases of COVID-19 here in NYC alone with over 24K deaths. Even those whose loved ones died from ailments and circumstances other than corona had their commemorations upended because of the need to practice safe behaviors for these times. Life the way we knew it has changed. We have changed. Some things have died. With creativity, imagination and adaptation other things have blossomed. We have learned that often less is more. What we really need, in addition to our health, is to walk the bridge of love that sustains us in pain, sorrow, joy and celebration.

Each time we say the *Sh'ma,* we speak of love. We are to love Gd with all our heart, all our soul and all our strength. And these words Gd commands us, for which we are responsible shall be *al l'vavcha*/on our heart. Why do we place holy words and instruction **on** our heart? Why not store them *balev*/**in** the heart? The Kotzker Rebbe says we pile words upon the heart so that when the heart inevitably breaks open, the words, prayers and instruction to pay attention and connect will fall in. Nothing, he taught, is so whole as a broken heart. Hearts, it seems, are meant to be broken just as they are meant to expand and spill over. But the heart in Judaism is not the sole source of love. It is the seat of wisdom. Love is deeper than the heart. In fact, the rabbis understand *hesed*/compassion as true love. A community of hesed takes responsibility for all in its midst. A loving community helps ensure a sense of being alive. To love in Judaism is to live.

Throughout these holy days, we offer the *shlosh esreh middo*t, the 13 Attributes of Gd, over and over again. *Adonai, Adonai el Rachum v'Hanun Erech Apayim v'Rav Hesed V'Emet. Notzer Hesed la'Alafim. Noseh Avon VaFesha V'Hata'ah v'Nakeh. Holy One, merciful and compassionate, patient, abounding in love and truth, assuring love for thousands of generations, forgiving iniquity, transgression and sin, and granting pardon. Noseh/Forgiving.* This is *Adon HaSlichot*, the Gd of forgiveness. The one who helps fill the world with love. The word used for forgiveness, *Noseh*, is connected to *Nisuin*, the rabbinic word for marriage which also means lift up. The Holy One reminds us what it means to live a Gdly life. Loving our neighbor and loving ourselves demands trust and commitment. It requires a contract, a sacred covenant to remind us that we merit love, that we must know ourselves and know the other. Love means lifting up and helping to carry the weight of the other. Knowing what causes them pain. Love means reaching out to raise someone's spirit and help them feel seen. Tomorrow - or even this evening - send someone a meal, buy the person behind you at Starbucks or Breads some coffee. Send cards or crossword puzzles to seniors at Met Council. Arrange contactless delivery of flowers or challah to a friend for Shabbat. Set up a zoom tutorial or read someone a book. Bring more love into the world.

How much will you love in the year to come? How much will we love in the year to come?

Let us write this next chapter of love together, as builders of community, holding the essence of Habonim.

Rabbi Lisa Gelber *is rabbi, mother, marathon runner, spiritual director, breast cancer survivor and PELOTON enthusiast. She serves as Advisory Committee member of BFOR: The BRCA Founder Outreach Study (BFORStudy.com) and speaks nationwide about domestic violence in faith community. Lisa sits on the Executive Council of the Rabbinical Assembly and the NYBR Board of Governors. She was featured in the Emmy Nominated Documentary ALL OF THE ABOVE: Single, Clergy, Mother. Lisa fills her days as spiritual leader of Congregation Habonim on the Upper West Side of Manhattan where she lives with her daughter and Torah muse, Zahara.*

THE COURAGE TO CALL OUT

Rabbi Maya Y. Glasser

Min Ha-meitzar karati Yah, Anani b'merchav Yah

From the depths, I called out to God; God answered me from a vast expanse.

Min ha-meitzar... from the depths, we've called out... what is this virus? Why is this happening to us? How do we best protect ourselves and our families? How do we navigate this unprecedented situation? How can we put one foot in front of the other, physically and metaphorically, as our lives have been altered and routines destroyed, as time blends together in a series of days, weeks, months sheltering in place and covering our faces?

For many long months, we've been stuck in the depths. We've been constricted. We've been trapped in our living spaces. We've been ensconced in fear about a new and mysterious virus that has no cure.

Our ancestors, too, found themselves caught in unimaginable situations, feeling alone and crying out to God. We are the newest links in the chain of those stuck in the depths, doing our best to navigate the unique circumstances of our day, and calling out to be seen in our struggles. We are like Sarah, calling out for a child, like Joseph crying for help from the pit his brothers threw him in; we are like Miriam desperately wanting someone to save her people.

THE COURAGE TO CALL OUT

In yesterday's Haftarah portion, we read the story of Hannah. Hannah is another brave soul from our tradition, who felt constricted because of her circumstances. She was unable to have children. Hannah becomes bitter to the core, weeping and bargaining with God. She calls out from the depths- but no one around her can understand her. They do not truly listen, and so cannot respond to her in the way that she needs. Her husband wonders why he isn't enough. And her clergy, the priest Eli, does not take the time to get to know her before judging her and making assumptions. The text reads, "Though her lips were moving, her voice could not be heard." Hannah's deepest prayers are blocked, because no one even tries to see her clearly. The intentions of her heart are pure, but she is disconnected from others. *Min Ha-meitzar karati Yah*, from the depths she calls out to God, but even those around here do not answer.

How familiar is Hannah's story to us this year. Her bitterness, weeping and bargaining probably have taken place in many of our households over the past months. And most of all, we, too, are blocked from communicating. Like Hannah's, our lips are moving… but covered by masks, they cannot be seen. We are blocked from viewing one another's faces. Even as we all cry out, we are impeded from true connection with one another. It is hard to hear, and hard to be heard.

When our faces are hidden from each other, we feel less human. We smile at someone in a supermarket, and realize they cannot see it, so it just looks like we're staring. Our mouths are obscured in photos, and it is difficult to converse in a normal tone.

THE COURAGE TO CALL OUT

Those who are hard of hearing or read lips have to find other ways to understand the people around them. Life feels unfamiliar when we are covered up. We have had to find new ways to communicate, new ways to call out to and answer one another.

Even our peoples heroes had to navigate similar challenges. When Moses first communicated with God, it was through a burning bush. Moses, too, was forced to leave his homeland and thrust into an unknown wilderness. When he sees flames bursting out of a plant that was not consumed, he, too, hides his face. He is afraid to look at God. When he asks God who and what God is, God responds: *"ehyeh asher ehyeh"*... "I will be what I will be." Moses feels small, and afraid. When he calls out from a place of fear, God answers. God answers in a way that shows that the future is unknown... it will be what it will be.

Yet, Moses is not alone. Moses, humble and scared, hiding his face, is suddenly connected to something bigger than himself. He has the courage to follow God's lead, and then, in turn, Moses, too, can be who he is. *Min Ha-meitzar karati Yah*- Amidst deep fear and uncertainty, he leads the Israelites from the narrow straits of slavery, from the depths of doubt, into the vast expanse, the open air of freedom.

And, this act of going from the constricted place to the wide one, earns him a special relationship with God. The Torah tells us that as the people were wandering in the desert, Moses would speak with God *"panim el panim"*, face to face, as one person does with another. Seeing God, and one another, face to face is the holiest interaction that we can have. Moses' journey from the narrow depths to the vast expanse, his deep faith, and his trust in not only God, but himself, leads him to this most sacred communication.

Hannah, too, eventually makes her way out of the depths. God sees her, and rewards her with what she wants most in the world. Because of her devout connection to her own self and to her God, Hannah continues to be herself and pray in the way that she needs to. Her conviction, and her preservation, her hope, lead her into the vast expanse.

How can we have that kind of faith? Both Hannah and Moses had the strength and courage to be themselves, even when they felt alone, and were convinced that no one was listening to them. The first step is to be open to the self-reflection that this time in the Jewish calendar demands of us. It is our task to identify what constricts us, what traps us in the narrow places. Maybe it is something out of our control. Maybe it is not. Maybe a habit is constricting us, or a relationship with someone who does not support us in the right ways. Maybe we are scared. Maybe we have not even contemplated the ways that we are stuck in the depths. Rosh Hashanah is a great time to start.

In a High Holiday poem called "Who By Fire: A Poem of Doubt and Return", Rabbi Patrick A. Beaulier writes,

> Holiness dwells in this day
> and our souls are overwhelmed.
> As a mirror reflects our image,
> this day reflects our Being.

THE COURAGE TO CALL OUT

In Truth, we open ourselves to
judgment:
to the All Knowing,
the Witness,
Remembering the knowledge, lost.

With honesty,
we stand before the open Book of
Remembrance
Which proclaims itself with arrogance,
And the seal of each person is there.
Mugshots of Divine Sparks,
Thumbprints on sacred scrolls.
The great shofar is sounded,
A still, small voice is heard.

And in our hearts we dust off the ever
forgotten poem,
And we wonder if it is true.
That on Rosh Hashanah it is inscribed,
And on Yom Kippur it is sealed:

When we call out to God's Name
We acknowledge our lack of
understanding.
And yet we pray:
Act for the sake of
Your Name!
And sanctify

Your Name!
Through those who sanctity
Your Name!

THE COURAGE TO CALL OUT

Was that for us?
Was that for You?
We called you Teshuvah,
Return,
For You desire us to return from our
path
And live.

And live. And live. And live.
And live. And live. And live.
And live.

And as You wait
for us.
So shall we,
So shall we,
So shall we
return to You

Like Hannah, and like Moses, each of us has a unique role to play in this life. We are on our own paths in the wilderness. Each of us has experienced our own constricting places, our own narrow depths. And we've had moments in which we make it to the vast expanses, moments in which we triumph, learn, and grow. But, there are also times when that does not happen. As the poem acknowledges, calling out can show our own lack of understanding. Sometimes, when we call out, we do not receive the answers we are looking for. This is both a universal shared experience, and a deeply unique and personal one. We feel alone, and desolate, each of us in our own way. Whether it is someone not truly listening to us, or a piece of cloth or cotton physically blocking our faces, there are always factors that inhibit us from feeling heard.

During this season, we come together to cry out. We draw strength from one another. Even as we are constricted behind our masks, we continue to do the hard work of being open- to those around us, to God, and perhaps most difficult to ourselves.

We remind ourselves that having faith is not the same as being sure of what is ahead... but having faith is the courage to reflect openly and honestly, to know somehow that we will make it from the narrow places to the vast expanse; the courage to even summon the strength to call out from the depths.

Min Ha-meitzar karati Yah, Anani b'merchav Yah

From the depths, I called out to God; God answered me from a vast expanse.

Rabbi Danielle Upbin writes that we say this verse during, "the moments that cry out for answers, for finding our way out to the other side. This verse is a vision of how we long to feel and how we long to be seen... The open space doesn't profess to solve our problems. It doesn't erase the root cause of our trouble. But it does provide us with the foundation to master our next step. It creates a safe-haven moment in which to reflect and prepare our way forward."

As we envision a world in which we feel safe and seen and heard, doing our best to build strong foundations as we navigate through life, part of our task is also to be someone who answers when we hear others call out. After God answers the psalmist from the vast expanse, the text continues, *Odecha ki anitani, Vatehi li liy'shu'a*, I will praise you because you have answered me, and you will be my salvation.

The psalm reaffirms for us that just hearing an answer to our deep cries can be our salvation. Just as God answers Hannah during her profound moment of prayer, and Moses as he flees from what has trapped him, we, too, have the power to provide that wide open space for others. Especially during this time of isolation, when we hear cries, mere responses can be incredibly powerful. Our answers have the ability to lift people up out of loneliness, from constricting places, and provide much needed company. When we respond, we can create sacred interaction. Even though we live in our own homes, behind masks, we do not have to be trapped in our own depths. Though we are covered up physically, we can continue to see people as they are, and meet in the most sacred way, face to face.

Eloheinu, v'elohei Avoteinu v'Emoteinu – our God, and God of our ancestors who also struggled, who felt despair, who cried out hoping to be answered, please hear our prayers this day. Help us to have hope and continue summoning the courage to call out.

May these High Holidays, these different, unique, strange High Holidays be a safe-haven moment for us during an extremely chaotic time. Though we know that we won't solve all of our problems, may our striving to return, to live anew, help us to be open with ourselves. And though we are trapped and constricted by a virus, may we be inspired- by Hannah, by Moses, by each other- to have the strength to be who we are, have faith, and continue to call out- to God, and to one another.

Rabbi Maya Y. Glasser *was ordained from the New York campus of Hebrew Union College-Jewish Institute of Religion in May of 2018 with their first-ever Certificate in Pastoral Care. She currently serves as Assistant Rabbi of Anshe Emeth Memorial Temple in New Brunswick, NJ, and as of Summer 2021 will be the Rabbi of Congregation Ahavath Chesed in Jacksonville, FL. Some of her favorite parts of being a rabbi are developing connections with congregants of all ages, learning and growing through classes, prayer and rituals, and constantly striving to make our ancient texts new again. Rabbi Glasser is a member of the CCAR (Central Conference of American Rabbis) and the WRN (Women's Rabbinic Network). She is pleased to be a part of the CCAR Committee on Worship and Practice, and the Editorial Board of their upcoming Mourning App. In her free time, Rabbi Glasser loves listening to show tunes, learning to knit, and praying for the New York Mets.*

I WILL BUILD AN ALTAR
FROM THE BROKEN PIECES OF MY HEART

Rabbi Dr. Elyse Goldstein

Yom Kippur, 1848. A cholera pandemic is sweeping through Eastern Europe. Millions have died. Rabbi Israel Salanter, head of the Musar yeshivas in Lithuania, stands at his pulpit on Yom Kippur morning with a piece of challah and a glass of wine in each hand. It is a crisis, and community health officials have recommended that eating is a way to stave off the illness. Rabbi Salanter recites kiddush and motzi in a full voice, and with tears in his eyes, proceeds to eat and drink in front of his entire congregation on Yom Kippur morning.

Rosh Hashana, 2020. A COVID pandemic has swept the world and way too many have died. I stand at my pulpit in my dining room, ring lights and cameras. It is a crisis, and community health officials have recommended we stay at home. I've cut out many of the most beautiful readings and songs to keep the service short enough to stave off screen fatigue. I am in front of my computer on a day I normally do not drive, use electricity or the phone. I invite my congregation to join me on zoom, and with tears in my eyes, I press record.

You do what you gotta do. You do what is hard and what is right and what will help. And as I see it, 7 months to even 7 years is a blip on the Jewish history scene, and we have done this adaptation routine before. Remember, when the temple was destroyed in 70 CE Judaism should gone out of business. But our ability to do what you gotta do saved us. That doesn't mean it doesn't hurt. That doesn't mean it isn't hard.

A 13th century *piyut* or poem for Rosh Hashana, of unknown authorship but called *Shir Hayichud*, ends with these powerful words: "*mizbe-ach evneh b'shibaron libi*: I will build an altar from the broken pieces of my heart."

You take the pieces of your dashed dreams and you build an altar with them.

Rosh Hashana 2020. If you don't have a cottage or friends with cottages it's been a long hot summer and maybe you haven't drunk Quarantinis laughing with friends in the backyard. Maybe you were furloughed or lost your job and CERB is ending. Maybe your grandkids live in the States and it's been nine months since you've seen them and they don't want to go on zoom anymore for visits. Maybe your kids are anxious about being back in school and they've been leaning heavily on you while you are trying to work from home. Maybe a loved one had to go to hospital and you couldn't be there beside them. Maybe you live alone and are feeling extra lonely.

Now of course it depends on your temperament. Maybe you are an introvert so you enjoyed the quiet alone time and the release from pressures to socialize. Maybe you aren't a planner, you like to live in the moment without a thought as to where your next winter vacation will be. Maybe you hate shopping and you're so glad to have everything delivered.

I WILL BUILD AN ALTAR
FROM THE BROKEN PIECES OF MY HEART

And there are what we've come to know and love as the "silver linings": the quiet of less planes overhead, cleaner air and water, engagement with our neighbours, increased support for local businesses, reaching out to and reconnecting with friends who don't live close by. Pivoting in a way that made it possible for the shul to thrive even with its doors closed. The incredible generosity of City Shul members and high holiday plus participants who gave so we could do this.

"*mizbe-ach evneh b'shibaron libi*": We have spent all summer building altars from the broken pieces of our hearts.

Most of us say when asked how we are doing "I'm fine…" After all I have food, a house, *and* toilet paper. But don't you just want to say sometimes "I'm struggling today, but I don't know why;" or "I'm just not sure how I feel." May Pang wrote in Medium at the end of April: "I'm going to coin a new word … The next time someone asks me how I'm feeling, I'm going to say, "I'm feeling Covish."

It is perfectly ok to feel Covish and even more perfectly ok to say you do. Because its likely we are all going to feel Covish for a while to come. And it's important for us to acknowledge that. Author and child psychiatrist Dr. Daniel Siegel has a therapeutic formula he uses with children that has nothing to do with COVID but I think can help us all. He calls it "name it to tame it" —say out loud what negative emotion you're experiencing in order to get some distance from it. Labeling a difficult emotional experience allows you to take the reins back, if only briefly. There is truth in our pain, and there is growth in our pain— but only if our pain first acknowledged. By using our human gift of language, he says, with someone who cares about us, we might actually be able to make some order out of the chaos. And we Jews don't go to a mountain top alone to name it, we do it in community and we do it on the holiest day of the year.

So we name it to tame it: shock, grief, disappointment, loneliness, fear, uncertainty. "Ambiguous loss" that's unclear and lacks a resolution. The inability to solve this problem.

We name it to tame it today, here on Rosh Hashana on zoom: while virtual Judaism has allowed us to visit big name synagogues across the world and learn with each other across Canada and celebrate simchas together and mark passings together with participants from all over the world, it comes with a spiritual price-tag: we miss the full-bodied Judaism that is generated by face-to-face engagement.

I name it to tame it: Disorientation, and religious changes needing to be made immediately. Loss of members because they don't use or like zoom. Loss of our shins—those fabulous 18 year old Israeli ambassadors who enrich our school and our shul in so many ways, who aren't coming this year. Bar and Bat Mitzvah families not having their relatives in person, and the kids not standing in front of us all reading from our Torah scroll. Kids who love our Hebrew school but simply cannot sit in front of any more screen. Staff exhaustion and burnout.

I WILL BUILD AN ALTAR
FROM THE BROKEN PIECES OF MY HEART

Our Torah portion today has us weep with Hagar as she sits far away from her son in order to not see his suffering. She turns to God and says "let me not see the boys death." The text says she sat a bowshot away—and that's much more than 6 feet. The Hasidic master *Haemek Dvar* comments that she did it for *him*—she moved away so her crying wouldn't worsen his condition— but Rashi says she did it for *her*—the more Ishmael grew close to death the farther away from him his mother moved. Unlike Abraham who in tomorrow's reading will *walk with* Isaac in his anxiety, Hagar "checks out" when the going gets tough. We haven't had that privilege, to sit it out far away, to check out from our anxious children and lonely parents and struggling friends.

Our Machzor seems to understand this. After literally naming all our fears about the ways we can die in *Unetaneh Tokef*—who by stoning, who by wild animals, who by thirst, who by *plague*, our prayer ends with a formula, three action tools to take it from a thing you know in your head to a thing you do in the world: *teshuva* (repentance), *tefila* (prayer) and *tzedakah* (charity). I am going to retranslate those three for this COVID year as:

Teshuva: from *lashuv*, to return: returning again to the teachings, the Corona Torah we learned during the worst part of the pandemic;

Tefila: the cultivation of hope and faith;

And **Tzedakah:** practicing charity on ourselves as well as others, by exercising enormous amounts of compassion this year.

These three will help us temper the severeness of the decree in this year of dashed expectations. These three are the ways we move forward from taming it to living with it.

First, Teshuva: let us return to the beautiful, deep Corona teachings of the early spring:

- The realization that we are fragile by ourselves and that our strength lies in being part of a community.

- That there are some in our society more fragile than others and we must actively rectify that

- That we have to learn to not be afraid of solitude and alone time.

- That we must value those closest to us.

- That going back to basics is healing.

- That we must pay attention to our own mental health and to the mental health of everyone around us, and.

- That slowing down is beneficial

Second, Tefila: Rabbi Jonathan Sacks writes, "to be a Jew is to be an agent of hope in a world serially threatened by despair…" Hope is not about getting what we want, things working out for the best, or escaping disaster just in the nick of time. Vaclav Havel, wrote: "Hope is a state of mind, not of the world…It's an orientation of the spirit…"

I WILL BUILD AN ALTAR
FROM THE BROKEN PIECES OF MY HEART

We must orient our spirits because we do not *find* hope— we *create* it. According to Viktor Frankl, Holocaust author of Man's Search for Meaning, "Everything can be taken from a man but one thing… – to choose one's attitude in any given set of circumstances."

The Hebrew word for faith is "emunah," and it means steadfastness. Faith does not require specific beliefs. Faith is the choice to remain steadfast in the face of uncertainty. Everyone on this screen today has shown faith in being here.

And **third, tzedakah**, compassion— for ourselves first and foremost, accepting that life is different right now and we are allowed to expect less of ourselves. (And *that* is very hard for a type A overachiever like me to say!) Compassion for others in surplus measures. Compassion for our shul by being patient and calm with the technological glitches that are bound to happen, by reaching out to the staff and checking in on us and by supporting our gargantuan programming efforts and online services by showing up. Compassion for our city: by continuing to do what we are supposed to do no matter how long or how inconvenient. Remember the old joke about how to get 50 Canadians out of a swimming pool? You simply say, "Please get out of the swimming pool." Well, the province said to us, "Please get out of the swimming pool" and we did so without being asked twice. We must continue to do that.

So we've named it. It's up to each of us to tame it. What new ways have emerged in this crazy time for you to nurture and grow? What once served you well that you are ready to let go of? What pieces of your life have you discovered are really "core" for you? And what will you do in the 10 days between Rosh Hashana and Yom Kippur to engage in *teshuva*, *tefila* and *tzedaka*? We move forward into the unknown with the only commitments we can really make this year: to reliving the hard lessons learned, to cultivating an attitude of faith and hope, and to an abundance of compassion. May this community be a source of strength for us in those commitments.

Shana Tova.

Rabbi Elyse Goldstein *is the founding Rabbi of City Shul in downtown Toronto. She served for twenty years as the Rabbinic Director of Kolel: The Adult Centre for Liberal Jewish Learning, an adult education institute she founded in 1991. She is the first woman elected as president of the interdenominational Toronto Board of Rabbis, and the past president of Reform Rabbis of Greater Toronto. She is the author of 4 books on women and Judaism. In 2005 she received the most prestigious award in Jewish education, the internationally recognized Covenant Award for Exceptional Jewish Educators, and was awarded Doctor of Laws Honouris Causis from Ryerson University in 2018 in recognition of her path-breaking work in Canada.*

TESHUVAH, TEFILAH, AND TZEDAKAH, OH MY!

Rabbinical Student Steven Gotlib

Just before Yom Tov, a good friend sent me a joke that "Jewish privilege is getting to end this rollercoaster of a year three months early." I chuckled as I read it, though I couldn't help but disagree. To me, one of the ideas I feel most privileged by in Judaism is one that we'll be reading quite frequently in the days to come.

וּתְשׁוּבָה וּתְפִלָּה וּצְדָקָה מַעֲבִירִין אֶת רֹעַ
הַגְּזֵרה:

But repentance, prayer and charity, remove the evil of the decree!

This deceptively simple line is one of the most iconic in all of the High Holy Days liturgy. On the surface, it is a very simple formula which needs no commentary. Even the *machzor* itself does not offer much aside from associating repentance with fasting, prayer with one's voice, and charity with money. ArtScroll editions of the *machzor* comment that this is "to indicate that sincere repentance includes fasting, prayer recited in a loud voice, and donations to charity."

I would like to offer a slightly different understanding of these three powerful words. Let's start with *t'shuvah*. Although many people tend to associate *t'shuvah* with fasting, this association is not inherent. The most oft-quoted definition of *t'shuvah* in the Jewish tradition,

offered by Maimonides, says nothing about the need
to fast:

וּמַה הִיא הַתְּשׁוּבָה. הוּא שֶׁיַּעֲזֹב הַחוֹטֵא חֶטְאוֹ
וִיסִירוֹ מִמַּחֲשַׁבְתּוֹ וְיִגְמֹר בְּלִבּוֹ שֶׁלֹא יַעֲשֵׂהוּ
עוֹד.

What constitutes *t'shuvah*? That a sinner
should abandon his sins and remove
them from his thoughts, resolving in his
heart, never to commit them again.

Rabbi Shlomo Zalman of Liady, the founding Rebbe of
Chabad Chasidism, also writes this clearly in his *Iggeret
Ha-T'shuvah*:

והנה מצות התשובה מן התורה היא עזיבת
החטא בלבד דהיינו שיגמור בלבו בלב שלם
לבל ישוב עוד לכסלה, למרוד במלכותו
יתברך ולא יעבור עוד מצות המלך, חס
ושלום, הן במצות עשה הן במצות לא תעשה
וזהו עיקר פירוש לשון תשובה: לשוב אל ה'
בכל לבו ובכל נפשו, לעבדו ולשמור כל
מצותיו... ולא כדעת ההמון שהתשובה היא
התענית

Now the *mitzvah* of repentance as
required by the Torah is simply the
abandonment of sin. This means that he
must resolve in perfect sincerity never
again to revert to folly, to rebel against
G-d's rule; he will never again violate the
King's command, G-d forbid, neither a
positive command nor a prohibition.
This is the basic meaning of the term

TESHUVAH, TEFILAH, AND TZEDAKAH,
OH MY!

> *t'shuvah* ("repentance") — to return to
> G-d with all one's heart and soul, to serve
> Him, and to observe all His
> commandments... This differs from the
> popular conception that repentance is
> synonymous with fasting on account of
> one's sins.

In other words, although fasting has for many become an integral part of feeling like they have repented and that perception has always been incredibly popular, Maimonides and the Alter Rebbe remind us that the core aspect of *t'shuvah* is not any physical action, but the internal resolution to improve ourselves. *T'shuvah* is not an act, but a thought.

On the other hand, many of us associate prayer as something we do internally, that ultimately needs no physical outlet in order to be efficacious. The *Shulchan Aruch*, however, codifies that prayer must be done loud enough for yourself to hear it:

> ולא יתפלל בלבו לבד אלא מחתך הדברים
> בשפתיו ומשמיע לאזניו בלחש ולא ישמיע
> קולו ואם אינו יכול לכוין בלחש מותר
> להגביה קולו וה"מ בינו לבין עצמו אבל
> בצבור אסור דאתי למטרד ציבורא:

> One should not merely think about the
> words of prayer in one's heart, but he
> must actually pronounce the words with
> his lips and cause them to be heard in a
> whisper tone in his own ears, however
> others should not hear his voice.

TESHUVAH, TEFILAH, AND TZEDAKAH, OH MY!

T'fillah, understood in this way, is all about speech.

Finally, we come to *tz'dakah;* charity. Giving charity is a concrete action that one performs. Together with *t'shuvah* and *t'fillah,* we now have examples of thought, speech, and action. Kabbalistic sources, quoted famously by the Tanya, describe these three paradigms as garments of the soul:

יש לכל נפש אלקית שלשה לבושים שהם
מחשבה דבור ומעשה

Each Divine Soul has three garments;
Thought, Speech, and Action

The elucidation of R. Yosef Wineberg adds that "just as garments give expression to their wearer's beauty and importance, so, too, when the soul dons and utilizes these "garments", its intellect and emotion find expression."

These three requirements are not necessarily meant to specifically avert a negative decree during the season of the High Holidays alone. Rather, I would suggest that exclaiming them just before our fates are written on Rosh HaShanna or sealed on Yom Kippur is really about setting ourselves up for the future. Repenting, praying, and fasting during this season are wonderful ways of demonstrating our desire to grow, but New Years' Resolutions are meant to continue into the New Year for longer than just a week and a half. Our thoughts, words, and actions are how our souls, intellects, and emotions find expression in the world. Whether those expressions

70

are positive or negative, good or evil, is up to us. When
we take the time to ponder them, and use them as a
vehicle to transport holiness rather than profanity into
our lives throughout the year, we prove that we have
truly internalized our commitments to ourselves, our
world, and our Creator.

In an essay entitled "The Vocation of the Cantor," Rabbi
Abraham Joshua Heschel tells the story of a Hasidic
Rebbe in Galicia, among whose adherents were
many *hazzanim.*

> "Their custom was to gather at the
> rabbi's court for the Sabbath which
> precedes Rosh Hashanah. At the end of
> their stay they would enter the rabbi's
> chamber and ask him for his blessing that
> their prayers on Rosh Hashanah be
> accepted into heaven. Once, the story
> goes, one of the hazzanim entered the
> rabbi's chamber immediately after the
> Sabbath to take leave of the rabbi. When
> the rabbi asked him why he was in such
> a hurry to leave, the hazzan replied, "I
> must return home in order to go through
> the Mahzor and to take a look at the
> notes." Thereupon the rabbi replied,
> "Why should you go through the
> Mahzor of the notes; they are the same as
> last year. It is more important to go
> through your own life, and take a look at
> your own deeds. For you are not the
> same as you were a year ago." The

TESHUVAH, TEFILAH, AND TZEDAKAH, OH MY!

hazzan was no longer in a hurry to leave."

I've been thinking about this story a lot over the past few days. Not only because I currently find myself about to serve as *shaliach tzibbur* and need to convince myself that it's okay to stop going through the *machzor* over and over again, but because this year, this is the story of all of us.

The *machzorim* in our hands are the same as they were last year, but we all find ourselves here as profoundly different men and women than we were last year. No one could have imagined the trials and tribulations faced this past year, and no one can predict what this new year will bring. The past has passed. But the future is yet to come. The pages are the same, but we are not the same people as we were a year ago. We have been profoundly changed by this past year, each in our own unique way.

These *machzorim* in our hands can act as our rear-view mirrors, allowing us to put the trials and tribulations of the past year into personal perspective and map out where we hope the future can take us. We are the mapmakers. The pages are the same, but we are different people than we were a year ago. This year, we are all that *hazzanim*.

"We are the music makers, and we are the dreamers of dreams." The music we make this year begins with the blasts of the Shofar that we are about to hear in just a few moments.

TESHUVAH, TEFILAH, AND TZEDAKAH, OH MY!

According to Rav Saadia Gaon, the blowing of the Shofar is meant to be a reminder of the prophetic calls to repentance given to our ancestors throughout history. We should be aware of the fact that *HaShem* communicated with us and displayed through prophecy His desire not for us to be punished, but for us to be perfected. The past has already happened, but the future is in our hands. The pages are the same, but we are different people than we were a year ago. Only we can choose whether or not to internalize the messages of *t'shuvah, t'filah, and tz'dakah*.

Let us use these High Holy Days to fuel us into redemption not only in the present, but in the future as well. May we all have a happy and sweet New Year.

Steven Gotlib *is a fourth-year semikha student at Yeshiva University's Rabbi Isaac Elchanan Theological Seminary (RIETS). He currently serves as rabbinic intern at Congregation Beth Abraham-Jacob in Albany, New York and as webmaster /social media manager for The Lehrhaus. Steven holds a BA in communication and Jewish studies from Rutgers University, a certificate in mental health counseling from RIETS in partnership with the Ferkauf Graduate School of Psychology, and a certificate in spiritual entrepreneurship from the Glean Network in partnership with Columbia Business School. He and his wife, Ruth Malkah Rohde, live in Fair Lawn, New Jersey.*

DISTANCE

Rabbi Daniel Greyber

I never dreamed of conducting a social or physical distanced funeral, unable to offer a handshake, much less a hug. One of you lost your mom a few months ago. You could not attend her funeral in Chicago. You were left in a netherworld, feeling sad but still unable to fully process her death without seeing the grave; forever denied the moment when the dirt hits the coffin, the painful but sound that signals for us - this is real. I must move on. Another one of you had a brother who died in New York. You too could not be there for the funeral. We gathered for a *shiva* minyan on zoom and when you spoke to us after the prayers, you said, "I just want to be hugged." You spoke a truth we all felt, but could not act upon.

I have watched over zoom as Artie Axelbank performed a bris with new parents alone in their home, or accompanied by just a family member or two. I've recited a new baby's name through a screen over a cup of kosher wine from my dining room, unable to join in the *seudat mitzvah* - the mitzvah meal of celebration for another child who has entered the covenant. I have waved through the window of our *beit midrash* at our *b'nei mitzvah*, smiling, trying to help them lead a congregation of friends and family on screens far away. Some of you brought cardboard cutouts of grandparents who could not attend. On walks around Trinity Park with our dog Delilah, another person approaches and I walk to the other side of the street. Or when running on East campus I make a wide circle around other runners to avoid coming too close. I take shallow breaths in the grocery store and stay focused on my list, trying to weave my way between fellow shoppers who signal danger. I return home exhausted from the stress. I yearned to go to protests to tell our black brothers and sisters, black lives matter, racism is an unmitigated evil, a sin with which our country has yet to reckon; Martin Luther King's dream feels farther away than ever, but friends said to me, "our community needs you healthy. You can't get sick," so I spoke out and reached out in other ways, but kept my distance. Distance - it feels like that's all there is these days, when what I want most is to feel close. The distance hurts.

Someone once said, "When they give you something for free, you're the product." Social media companies are now more valuable than oil companies; our attention is a value commodity. Algorithms designed to keep our attention work by filing our feeds with people who agree with us. We believe Facebook connects us to the wider world - that it closes the distance - when what it really does is show us a slice of the world that mirrors our own opinions. Russian hackers pit us against each other and the upcoming election will only fan the flames and drive us further apart. In her book Reclaiming Conversation, Sherry Turkle writes about how texting and device mediated communication makes it easier for us to be cruel to one another because we can avoid the consequences of our language, of the pain we inflict with unkind words. She writes about how face-to-face conversation teaches empathy; it heals us. But now even a face-to-face conversation is masked; more conversation than ever - even this sermon - is mediated through a screen. The distance hurts.

And God, well, maybe God seems very very far away. Isaiah says, "Seek the Lord where he is to be found, Call upon him when he is close" (Isaiah 55:6). Maimonides (Laws of Repentance 2:6) says repentance and prayer are always appropriate but the verse from Isaiah teaches that between "Rosh HaShanah and Yom Kippur it is even more appropriate and it is accepted immediately." In other words, The High Holiday period is when God can be found; now is when God is nearest." But, I imagine for many of us, as 5781 begins, God feels far away, distant.

The Israeli poet Rivka Miriam wrote a poem about distance that I hope might speak to us this Rosh Hashanah and give us some tools to find a way forward:

הַמֶּרְחָק שֶׁבֵּין נְקֻדָּה לִנְקֻדָּה, הוּא הִסְבִּיר
כָּמוֹהוּ כַּמֶּרְחָק שֶׁבֵּינִי לְבֵין עוֹרִי
וְשֶׁבֵּין הַכּוֹכָב לְאוֹרוֹ
כַּמֶּרְחָק שֶׁבֵּין הַחֹלִי לַבָּרִיא
שֶׁבֵּין הַכְּמִישָׁה לַצְּמִיחָה וְלַפְּרִי
שֶׁבֵּין הַמְדַבֵּר לְבֵין מָה שֶׁנִּהְיָה בִּדְבָרוֹ.

The distance between one point and another,
he explained,
is like the distance between me and my skin
or between a star and its light
like the distance between sickness and health
between withering and flowering and fruit
between the One who speaks and that which
exists through His speaking.

76

DISTANCE

First, the poet says all of what we are being taught about distance is something "he explained" - who is "he?" We get the sense he is not there anymore. Has he died? Does he now exist only as a memory? Or is he still alive but inaccessible? Were these the words he spoke before leaving on a trip during which he'd be unreachable? Or perhaps is the relationship over and she is remembering these words fondly? Or bitterly? We don't know - but even this teaching about distance is distant. And yet...

The poet begins by telling us that what we perceive as distance is like what's there between me and my skin - which is to say, no distance at all. Is there a "me" outside of my skin? I can look at my skin; sometimes some peels off - so it is not all of me, but it is part of me. Distance, she says, is like when we look up at the stars: is there a difference between the object called a star and the light we see when it finally arrives to earth? Up there, there is a star - there must be matter of some sort; fuel for the fire that burns that creates the light, but to us, there seems to be no difference at all - the star we know is just the light we see.

I stumbled over this next phrase. What does she mean: "like the distance between sickness and health?" I have been sick! I have had a fever. It may be hard for me to walk, to eat. There is a great distance between when I'm sick and when I'm healthy. When I'm healthy, I can swim and walk and move around. I called my friend and teacher, Rabbi Sager. He gave me the poem after all and in the past few months, he's been doing a lot of thinking about sickness and health. He said when you're sick, a lot of people relate to you as sick. Modern medicine has a lot of tests and monitors and scans to tell you about your disease. But we're less good at quantifying health, at measuring all the things we can still do, like write and teach and speak and pray and be surprised by the world each day. "I realize," he said to be, "I'm not going to walk vigorously around the Old City of Jerusalem again. I look back on that "me" with some nostalgia and perhaps sadness, but also with a sense of surprise and relief. Doing that used to be a part of my sense of self, of who I understood myself to be, a vigorous person who could walk the streets of Jerusalem. Now, even though that's gone, I am still here. There is an "I" who continues even while part of me is gone."

I think about our country and race and what we've been through this summer - our country feels sick. Over and over again we witness black men and women killed too quickly and easily and cruelly by police officers in America. The dream of racial equity feels so far away. But were we healthier before this summer? Or was acceptance of the status quo just a cancer growing inside us? Aren't the protests and the hard conversations of the past summer healthier than smothering silence? Didn't these move us closer to the dream of equality? The answer remains to be seen but the distance between sickness and health might be closer than we thought.

Our society is literally struggling with sickness. Coronavirus prevents us from gathering in stadiums and synagogues. We are not physically together this year; there is much to mourn, but we are not only alone; we are alone, together. This year, so many of the things that we depend upon to tell us it is the High Holidays - harmonizing together in the sanctuary; seeing old friends in the lobby; sitting in the seat we know; looking at our loved one's plaque on the memorial board - so many of those things are distant. But there is not only distance. Not only because we can listen on zoom as Eric Meyers chants Une Tane Tokef, or Jeff Derby reads the Torah. Not only because we can go and hear the shofar being blown tomorrow afternoon. But because though we are separated, we are still together, going through this difficult time together. We know other people feel lonely. We know other people yearn for the things we yearn for. We know other people care.

In the past six months as our society has struggled with sickness, I have discovered anew what is so healthy about our congregation. I've witnessed you staying up through the night to watch someone's body at a funeral home on your computer and meet in a zoom room to say the prayers for a *tahara* to continue our traditions that honor our loved ones who have died. You did those things just last night for long time congregant Barrie Bergman who was laid to rest this morning. I have seen you deliver challah and babka to each other's homes. I've seen you call and check up on each other and make minyan over zoom each Wednesday morning or in the evening for a shiva. Through the Rabbi's discretionary fund, we have given thousands of dollars to Porch Durham and the Durham Public School Foundation to help feed Durhams' children because children should never go hungry. I've seen you show up for church and send letters of love and support to The River, telling them black lives matter; telling them what they told us after Pittsburgh: "You matter. You are not alone." I've seen us partner with the Walltown Neighborhood

Ministries and fill our Friedman Center with food that has been distributed just outside our building every week this summer for the homeless and those most in need. There is health in this time of sickness. We have grown closer even as we are apart.

"Between withering and flowering and fruit" says the poet. Why not begin with "flowering" and end with "withering?" Isn't spring the beginning and fall the end? Or perhaps the poet is telling us nothing can sprout and grow until something else dies. That every death is a beginning, and every beginning includes an ending of something else. In the Torah reading this morning, we read that Hagar

> went off and sat at a distance, about a
> bowshot away, for she thought, "I cannot
> watch the boy die." And as she sat there,
> she began to sob.

She walked away. There was distance between her and her baby. He was withering before her eyes. And then, perhaps only then,

> God heard the boy crying, and the angel
> of God called to Hagar from heaven and
> said to her, "What is the matter, Hagar?
> Do not be afraid; God has heard the boy
> crying as he lies there. Lift the boy up and
> take him by the hand, for I will make him
> into a great nation." Then God opened
> her eyes and she saw a well of water. So
> she went and filled the skin with water
> and gave the boy a drink.

The water was there before, but only with distance, with letting go could she see that the well had been there all along. How appropriate Rosh Hashanah comes in the Fall as the leaves begin to dry up and wither. The distance between the withering of autumn and the blossoming of spring is no distance at all.

"between the One who speaks and that which exists through His speaking." This final phrase—*sh'hakol nihiyah bi'dvaro* - is from a blessing we say, thanking God for even the tiniest morsel of nourishment. For a sip of water or tea. The distance between God - the One who speaks - and the most insubstantial part of God's world seems so vast. But haven't we been reminded this year how small the world is; how connected we are, not only to the people we see on the street, but as a society, as a country, even with those across the world, and to the Oneness of creation. Perhaps we can find God again not by going on a journey, but through the gift of solitude and stillness these days of quarantine have provided.

The distance hurts. It is real and as much as I wish I had an answer, I don't know when it's going to end. But the pain is not all there is. In a searing letter to his granddaughter after the death of his daughter, her mother, Leonard Fein wrote, "I want for you, my love, flesh of my flesh and bone of my bone, that you will be whole. The emptiness cannot be wished away, nor is there reason to try. All we need guard against is the swelling of the emptiness, its displacement of the other truths of our lives. You are the daughter of a mother who died just 500 days after you were born. But for sure her story did not end in January of 1996. Her death is a sorry fact of your life – but not, I pray, the defining fact.

There is much, much more to her story than the tragedy of her death – and all that is yours, too." There is light to be found in darkness, health in sickness, renewal in withering. As we celebrate the creation of the world this year, may we never feel distant from the One who brought us into being. Let us "call upon God while She is close," now, and always. Amen.

Daniel Greyber *is rabbi at Beth El Synagogue in Durham, North Carolina, author of* **Faith Unravels: A Rabbi's Struggle with Grief and God**, *and currently in cohort VII of the Rabbinic Leadership Initiative of the Shalom Hartman Institute in Jerusalem. Greyber served as Team USA Rabbi at the 19th and 20th World Maccabiah Games in Israel. Formerly a Jerusalem Fellow at the Mandel Leadership Institute, a faculty member at the Ziegler School of Rabbinic Studies in Los Angeles, and the Executive Director of Camp Ramah in California, Rabbi Greyber's articles have been featured in a wide range of Jewish publications.*

HOPE AS A PARTICIPATORY VIRTUE: EVEN NOW, ESPECIALLY NOW, ESSENTIALLY NOW

Rabbi Stephanie Kolin

At the very beginning of this pandemic, the very first thing that happened in my family is that I broke my toe and probably my foot. I had just heard the news that we would be quarantined for two weeks – which, at the time, was shocking. I leapt out of my chair and ran to check the medicine cabinet to ensure we had enough over the counter toddler meds, and in doing so, I kicked a piece of furniture so hard that I nearly passed out. I'm actually surprised you didn't hear me screaming.

Purple-footed, I thought then that my metaphorical story of this pandemic would be my broken foot that broke on the day our country broke and healed by the end of the quarantine, a dramatic story of panic, pain, and a process toward wholeness again. A story that embodied HOPE above all.

Two weeks slipped into eight weeks and finally I could walk again, but as we know now, by then, COVID numbers were surging and people were dying. My tidy little narrative was meaningless. Eight weeks became three months, bled into five, and now six. In that time, schools closed, our kids struggled with virtual learning, desperately missing their friends, and working parents endured the utterly unsustainable. In that time, George Floyd, an unarmed black man, was murdered with a knee on his neck and protestors took to the streets. In that time, people lost their jobs, some went hungry. Loneliness was so thick we could touch it.

Our community lost beloved members and could not mourn together in person. In that time, we learned of intentional misinformation and deception from our government that cost lives, and a presidential campaign began and was bloody with white supremacy before the nominating conventions were over. In that time, we lost some of our greatest advocates for truth and justice in Representative John Lewis and Justice Ruth Bader Ginsberg. Yes, we flattened curves because we love each other and yes, we moved our spiritual community to these screens, refusing to lose the tether between us. But In that time, things seemed to keep breaking, each day harder than the one before it.

I thought the poetry of this virus would rise and fall with a story of breaking and healing, but here we still are, standing in the unknown of COVID, the unknown of an increasingly alarming political moment heading into an already contested election. It is a perfect storm of crises, and the ending is still unwritten.

And I came here to talk with you about hope. Especially on this day that is our new year – we crave it, we need it. But hope is a tricky thing. Our tradition – really, most faith traditions – are full of texts that posit hope or try to instill hope. In our Psalms, we read – "we go to sleep crying, but joy comes in the morning."[5] We sing "those who sow in tears will reap in joy."[6] We learn a midrash

---

[5] Psalm 30:5
[6] Psalm 126:5

of Adam and Eve on their very first day on earth. They are so afraid as the sun goes down. It gets darker and darker and they are terrified, thinking maybe the sun won't come back. But at the break of dawn, the sun rises again. And they are calmed and relieved and grateful.[7]

And we want that. That guarantee that the sun will rise again, the darkness will give way to the light, and joy will come in that morning. We want to believe there is an "other side" to this and it's coming. Soon and almost and just over that hill.

But there's a problem with that kind of hope. As I sat typing these words, a headline popped up that said: "CDC tells states to prepare for COVID-19 Vaccine by Nov 1" and I felt the familiar rollercoaster of "getting my hopes up" and the impending spiral of deep disappointment when it turns out not to be true. Our desire to believe in the next flicker of light is so strong that it also has the power to break us.

Hope is the thing that lets us take the next step forward when things are at their darkest. What do we do when it seems to slip through our fingers over and over?

I was recently introduced to something called the Stockdale Paradox.[8] It's named for Admiral James

---

[7] Avodah Zarah 8a

[8] I am so grateful to my friend Robin, and her co-author, for writing this brilliant article, from which I am trying to draw deeply in this moment. "What the Stockdale Paradox Tells us About Crisis Leadership," by Robin Abrahams and Boris Groysberg, Aug 17, 2020. https://hbswk.hbs.edu/item/what-the-stockdale-paradox-tells-us-about-crisis-

Stockdale, who was held hostage during the Vietnam War. Having survived horrible conditions for 7.5 long years, not knowing if or how he'd survive, he was asked what gave him the strength to come out on the other side. And he said "I never lost faith in the end of the story.

I never doubted not only that I would get out, but also that I would prevail in the end and turn the experience into the defining event of my life . . ." But he continued. When he was asked about those who did not make it out of the camps, he said: "The optimists," . . . "they were the ones who said, 'We're going to be out by Christmas.' And Christmas would come, and Christmas would go. Then they'd say, 'We're going to be out by Easter.' And Easter would come, and Easter would go. And then Thanksgiving, and then it would be Christmas again. And they died of a broken heart. He said: "You must never confuse faith that you will prevail in the end, which you can never afford to lose, with the discipline to confront the most brutal facts of your current reality, whatever they might be."

This is the paradox he used to get through the hardest time in his life. "To have faith, but to confront reality."[9] To name how hard this is. How it sucker-punches us right in the gut over and over. But to believe we will prevail, we will come out of this time. Not to believe with an optimism that can manipulate our emotions but with something more. And this, we might call hope.

---

leadership?fbclid=IwAR0I6Et6MBw6PtMWthITnJnQdEIdXozmW0eoth8WJLRfG2Z2g9uPyAbrqTs
[9] Ibid.

HOPE AS A PARTICIPATORY VIRTUE

Rabbi Jonathan Sacks teaches: "Optimism is the belief that things are going to get better. Hope is the belief that we can make things better. Optimism is a passive virtue, hope is an active one. It takes no courage, he says, to be an optimist, but one does need courage to hope." "No Jew," he continues, "knowing what we do of the past, of hatred, bloodshed, persecution in the name of God . . . can be an optimist. But Jews have never given up hope."[10]

We are challenged to be an active participant in our own salvation. It's not an easy ask, especially in such difficult times. But we have a context for this flavor of hope.

In 70 CE, Jerusalem and the Temple were destroyed by the Roman army. All of Jewish life happened in that city and that Temple. This catastrophe could have meant the end of the Jewish people. Many died, but one guy, Rabbi Yochanan Ben Zakkai, fled. He ran to a place called Yavneh and he built there a school. And he and the sages re-imagined Judaism into the religion and people that we know today. Animal sacrifice, which they couldn't do anymore, became prayer as we know it. They morphed our reliance on holy space, which was gone, into holy time, which we and all of the diaspora know as Shabbat.

Rabbi Yochanan could have very understandably given up. Or he could have said – wait, I'm sure a better day is coming soon! But instead, he looked at the utterly brutal thing he was facing, he grieved deeply all that was lost, and then he chose to take action. And when he

---

[10] Rabbi Jonathan Sacks, *The Dignity of Difference*

was at his lowest, he still believed his actions could make a difference.

It may have been the hardest thing he ever did. It will surely be among the hardest things we ever do.

In many ways, we are facing a Jerusalem that's breaking. With multiple and intersecting crises of COVID, systemic racism and the rise of White Supremacy and anti-semitism, economic distress and ecological disaster, loss of trust in our government and institutions, and unprecedented challenges in our own homes.

Where are you feeling it most? It's alright to name our most brutal truths.

A brutal truth in our country is a systemic racism that does massive violence to our Black family and neighbors. Optimism might have us say – ya know, maybe we wanted to believe we were in a post-racial America. We had a Black president – maybe things were just getting better on their own.

But centuries of entrenched inequality don't just get better. It takes a sustained set of ongoing actions by people committed to dismantling racism. So where is the hope in that? Radical hope is us making a commitment to do that hard work and believing that our work will ultimately bring about an anti-racist society. That would be hope.

A brutal truth is that we are in a terrifying political moment in our fragile democracy. The stakes are so high. Higher now than they were 24 hours ago.

Optimism would be to believe that we'll wake up on November 4th and it will just all turn out okay. This is why optimism is not only enticing, but also dangerous. It abdicates our role in critically important moments. Hope, however, is believing that our actions now **can** set us on a different course. The single most powerful demonstration of hope today might be helping to make sure that every person has the right and ability to vote in this election – that would be an extraordinary act of hope.

Maybe the brutal truth you're facing is the pain or loneliness your kids or your parents are going through, or your own broken heart as you sit exhausted in this depleting moment. What does hope look like for you? What actions – even small ones – could you take that you believe might make a difference? Will you choose to laugh more with your friends? Will you seek out nature and break open to its inspiration or a therapist and break open to yourself? Will you make food at a soup kitchen? Call a neighbor who's suffering? Love bigger and more radically than you ever have before? Because that, too, is the hope of resilience, of resistance, of creating a new world in the midst of the pain of this one.

Today, on Rosh Hashanah, our new year, we pray: Hayom Harat Olam.[11] This is the day the world is born anew. Can you believe that – today – even on the hardest Rosh Hashanah we've seen in some time – we still declare that we have conceived of a new world, a new reality, and it is right now being born! But in this

---

[11] Traditional Rosh Hashanah liturgy, found in the shofar service

prayer, it's not a passive birth. We are named as actors in helping it emerge – we ask God to lead us toward *chen,* acts of grace, toward *mishpat,* acts of justice, and toward *kedushah,* acts of holiness that elevate our lives. Our actions will it into existence. It is not easy to birth a new world. It is not easy to participate in our own salvation, when some days, we feel like we're just getting by.

And yet, as the author, Rebecca Solnit, writes: "We have more to do and doing it is itself a way to assuage despair, misery, fear. Hope, she teaches, matters most when it's hardest."[12] Hope, even now, especially now, essentially now. If we can find the well springs of courage to name how very hard this all is, and to still be able to say out loud to one another that our actions can, might, do, make a difference, if we can count ourselves on each other's team for what lies ahead – then we have already chosen hope.

That is the joy that comes in the morning. *That* is the sun that rises again. It's in us, such that together, in time, we will rise out of these hardest days, we will care for one another in life-giving ways, and we will build something better, light out of darkness.

May the year ahead be gentler on us, be sweeter for us and those we love, truly for all people. May this be a year of true hope.

---

[12] From her Facebook post on September 12, 2020

Shanah tovah U'metukah.[13]

Rabbi Stephanie Kolin *is the rabbi of Union Temple of Brooklyn. Through this pandemic, in partnership with UT's lay leadership and our new family at CBE, Rabbi Kolin has guided the Union Temple community through a merger with Congregation Beth Elohim and will join the CBE clergy team. Rabbi Kolin was ordained from the Hebrew Union College NY campus in 2006 and has, since then, served as a rabbi of Temple Israel in Boston, as the Co-Director of Just Congregations and co-founder of Reform-CA (now RAC-CA, a statewide campaign of the Reform Movement for a more just and compassionate California), and as a rabbi of Central Synagogue in Manhattan. Stephanie lives in Brooklyn with her wife and their awesome almost four-year-old daughter.*

---

[13] An overall gratitude and acknowledgement: I want to thank Rabbis Joshua Lesser, Michael Adam Latz, Oren Steinitz, Rabbi Shira Koch Epstein, and Cantor Cheryl Wunch for their rigorous and generous sharing of ideas and teachings on hope, and Rabbis Dara Frimmer and Asher Knight for their wise and hilarious "*chevruting.*"

BREATHE

Rabbi Michael Adam Latz

A few days after George Floyd (z"l), our neighbor, was murdered, Floyd's six year old daughter Gianna, was foisted high upon the shoulders of a family friend to look out upon the growing memorial at 38th and Chicago (the site of Floyd's murder).

Gazing upon the thousands of protestors who gathered night after night, young Gianna proclaimed with heartbreaking pride, "Daddy changed the world!"

I remember hearing those words and in those wrenching days, looking at the people around me—so many of you were there, on the streets, wearing your masks, holding signs, supporting each other, crying out for human dignity, our shattered hearts laid out on the pavement like broken glass. I saw your eyes, your tears, your rage, your longing, your terror, your grief.

There is something so human about feeling so broken-hearted, so raw, so angry, and so vulnerable all at the same time!

Layla Saad, the author of *White Supremacy and Me*, writes, "Without those feelings, nothing changes, because there is no reason to heal what does not feel broken. I invite you not to run away from the pain but to let it break your heart open... there is no clean, comfortable or convenient way to dismantle a violent system of oppression. You must roll up your sleeves and get down into the ugly, fertile dirt."

The ugly dirt, fertilized with blood and tears, haunted by the echoes of a man who cried out over and over, **"I can't breathe. I can't breathe."**

Rabba Tamar Elad Applebaum, my beloved rabbi and friend, teaches in the name of Rebbe Nachman. He states that the purpose of the Torah and *t'filah* (prayer) are to teach us to breathe[14].

So we could learn how to breathe between the words, that our souls would vibrate with life.

In Hebrew, one of the words for soul is *nefesh*. Nefesh in Torah also means, "throat." It is in our throat where the work of our lungs meets the oxygen of the outside world and in a scientific and spiritual wonder, the alchemy of human life hums.

But not for George Floyd.

Or Breonna Taylor.

Not for Eric Garner.

Or Philando Castille.

Not for Tamir Rice.

---

[14] https://www.hartman.org.il/intervention-in-times-of-crisis-on-moral-and-spiritual-leadership/

BREATHE

Or Sandra Bland.

Not for Mike Brown, Jr.

Or Ahmaud Arbery.

Or Daniel Prude.

Zichronam Livracha.

The breath of their lives was literally choked out of their bodies, by knees and bullets and centuries of racism and racist systems that land with the force of history on Black and Brown and Native bodies.

Systemic racism is literally choking the breath out of human being's bodies. It isn't even the only force and crisis stealing our breath.

Our breathing is not easy in a time of COVID19, where the virus itself combined with the virus of virulent incompetency of the Trump administration has literally choked the life out of more than 200,000 Americans, choked off economic progress and financial sustainability for millions of unemployed people, and choked the breath out of children and their parents, desperate to go back to school but legitimately afraid for their lives if they do.

Our breath is at risk by raging fires and devastating hurricanes, a climate in peril and failed leadership in Washington who call this calamity a hoax, who refuse to listen to scientists, whose obscene greed has seemingly cut off the flow of oxygen to their brains and their hearts.

Our breath is smothered by the epidemic of gun violence, compounded by the epidemics of homophobia and transphobia, Islamophobia and antisemitism and the white nationalists who harass, brutalize, and kill our neighbors.

There is no more precious nor precarious human right than the right to breathe.

We long for a day a when all our neighbors, our children, our parents can breathe free.

The Torah that we will soon hear chanted has within it a moment of perilous breathlessness. After a three-day journey, Abraham has bound his beloved son Isaac upon a mountain top altar. His knife wielding hand is raised over his child. Called by God to sacrifice his son, Abraham appears to have every intention of going through with the repugnant deed.

וַיָּבֹ֗אוּ אֶֽל־הַמָּקוֹם֮ אֲשֶׁ֣ר אָֽמַר־ל֣וֹ הָאֱלֹהִים֒ וַיִּ֨בֶן
שָׁ֤ם אַבְרָהָם֙ אֶת־הַמִּזְבֵּ֔חַ וַיַּעֲרֹ֖ךְ אֶת־הָעֵצִ֑ים
וַֽיַּעֲקֹד֙ אֶת־יִצְחָ֣ק בְּנ֔וֹ וַיָּ֤שֶׂם אֹתוֹ֙ עַל־הַמִּזְבֵּ֔חַ
מִמַּ֖עַל לָעֵצִֽים:

They arrived at the place of which God had told him. Abraham built an altar there; he laid out the wood; he bound his son Isaac; he laid him upon the altar.

BREATHE

וַיִּשְׁלַח אַבְרָהָם אֶת־יָדוֹ וַיִּקַּח אֶת־הַמַּאֲכֶלֶת
לִשְׁחֹט אֶת־בְּנוֹ:

And Abraham picked up the knife to slay his son[15]

In that terrifying moment, an arm raised to the heavens, a child bound upon the altar of his father's grotesque and misguided faith, we are left gasping.

But there is a lead up to this moment that often gets overlooked. And this verse of Torah teaches us a great deal about how we got to this place of breathlessness — and what we need to do to create a world where everyone can breathe free.

Abraham built an altar.

He laid out the wood.

He bound his son Isaac.

He laid him upon the altar.

And then he picked up the knife.

At each of those moments Abraham could have stopped. In fact, the Medieval commentator Rashi asks: Why does the text say that Abraham and Isaac arrived at Mount Moriah on the third day of their journey?

"Why did he not see [the mountain] immediately? In order that people could not later say, "The command

---

[15] Gen 22: 9-10

96

shocked and confused him and muddled his thinking; had he had time to think about it, he would not have gone ahead with it." (Rashi, Gen. 22: 4) Had the Akeda not taken place on the third day, one might have concluded that Abraham acted out of a momentary lapse of his senses, out of a surge of religious ecstasy."[16]

Rashi is clear: Abraham knew what he was doing.

At each of the moments that officers held their knees on George Floyd's (z"l) neck they could have stopped. They had eight minutes and 47 seconds to stop. To let him breathe. To let him live. They failed.

At each of the moments the President and his cronies called COVID19 a hoax, at each of the moments public health officials warned this pandemic was fatal and spread rapidly, at each of the moments the President and the Republican Senate blocked legislation for mass public testing, for adequate PPE, they could have stopped and done the right thing. They failed.

At each of the moments in the past 40 years, leaders in Washington who could have advanced gun safety legislation and made a measurable impact on the lives of every human in this nation, they could have stopped, voted, and done the right thing. They failed.

No one gets bound and placed upon the altar by accident. COVID19 did not create vast inequality in our society; it simply exposed the intertwined inequities of racism, poverty, the climate crisis, sexism, gun violence,

---

[16] *When God is Near: On the High Holidays* by Yehuda Amital

white nationalism, and the rightwing asphyxiation of vital public services and our social safety net—inequities that have existed for decades, especially for People of Color.

The truth is that we won't unbind our society and be able to collectively breathe by accident or happenstance, by dumb luck or a mythic angel.

To loosen the knots around our throats so that we can all breathe requires intentional, thoughtful intervention. It requires moral leadership. It requires each of us pause in this New Year to ask questions to help ourselves and our community breathe:

How will we treat each other with empathy and compassion?

How will we transform where possible and dismantle where necessary the systems that choke our neighbors to death?

How will we build new systems that allow our neighbors to breathe free?

Centuries of systemic racism and militarized training of the police and repugnant character went into the men and the moment that murdered our neighbor, George Floyd (z"l).

So did a lack of moral imagination. We must dream together a world in which the conversation about public safety holds at its center everyone's fundamental right to breathe.

And those of us who are white have the responsibility to listen to our beloved community members of color and take seriously their claims about how our current public safety system has harmed and failed them.

We must explore not just public policy to address the climate crisis—and yes, we must do that; we also need to imagine together what a world would look like where everyone treasures the planet, the mountains, the seas and support our youth leaders in this massive and essential project of climate justice.

We need to imagine not just a world without suffocating gun violence, but a world in which everyone is cared for.

We need to imagine a world where scientists and public health officials set policies for how we address fatal viruses and work with our communities to enable us to breathe, socialize, work, and be together.

Abraham's grave mistake was not merely that he reflexively followed God's command to sacrifice Isaac. Abraham's mistake was that he was in a mindset of apathy, indifference, order, and compliance. His mistake was not stopping long enough to interrogate the powerful voice commanding him to commit an act that contradicted everything he knew to be good and true.

Abraham's mistake was failing to pause long enough to realize that any God who asked him to sacrifice his son was no God worth believing in!

Our mistake would be to distance ourselves from Abraham and say, "We would never do something like that!" To address these interrelated mass crises, we have to take responsibility ourselves.

Now, I know that none of us willingly binds our children upon an altar. No white person at Shir Tikvah dons a white hood.

But in our passivity to accept the status quo, in our privileging of order over justice, we permit these travesties to take place.

In the Torah, we don't hear Abraham's internal dialogue; we have no idea how he's reckoning with any of it—if he is at all.

But *we* can know. We can verbalize what Abraham cannot. The first step to unbinding ourselves and our community from the altar of our indifference is to talk, to name, to discuss, to expose the ways we as individuals, as a congregation, as a city, as a nation, as a planet—through our action and our inaction—have cut off our neighbor's ability to breathe.

The conversations we must have are not the last step on the road to redemption; they are the first.

Isaac was saved by an angel. We cannot wait for mythic angels to save us. We must do that work ourselves.

It is up to each one of us to be the ones who embody that angel, to intervene, and to cry out: STOP! This is not working! This is immoral! Every human being deserves to breathe free!

And then we must do the holy work to dramatically reimagine together a new world of justice, equity, and human dignity into being.

The Akeidah concludes with Abraham naming the place where he sacrifices the ram in Isaac's stead as *"Adonai Yireh,"* the place where God sees. Indeed, our cities must be transformed into communities where each of us notices those who struggle to breathe and where every one of us intervenes until every human being— especially our Black and Brown and Native beloveds— lives and thrives with justice and dignity.

I close with one of America's greatest moral imaginators, Emma Lazarus. In her poem, "The New Colossus," Lazarus helps us imagine being in the world with expansive breath, her words etched into the Statue of Liberty, welcoming every human who comes to our shores. Lazarus' aspirational words are not yet real. Imagine what the world will look like if we make them so:

> Not like the brazen giant of Greek fame,
> With conquering limbs astride from land to land;
> Here at our sea-washed, sunset gates shall stand
> A mighty woman with a torch, whose flame
> Is the imprisoned lightning, and her name
> Mother of Exiles.
> From her beacon-hand
> Glows world-wide welcome;
> her mild eyes command

BREATHE

The air-bridged harbor that **twin cities** frame.
"Keep, ancient lands, your storied pomp!"
cries she With silent lips.
"Give me your tired, your poor,
Your huddled masses yearning to breathe free,
The wretched refuse of your teeming shore.
Send these, the homeless, tempest-tost to me,
I lift my lamp beside the golden door!"[17]

Shanah Tovah. May 5781 be a year we all breathe free.

As always, my deepest gratitude to Rabbi Dr. Lisa Grushcow, my chevruta, my colleague, my friend; Abbie Shain and Lyonel Norris for offering sensitive, clear, and powerful feedback; my children, Noa and Liat, whom I love to the end of the universe and back again, and Michael Simon, my husband, whose keen eye and piercing questions make me a better rabbi, husband, and father.

---

[17] https://thehistoricpresent.com/2019/09/21/give-me-your-poor-your-tired-your-huddled-masses-yearning-to-breathe-free/

BREATHE

Michael Adam Latz *is dad to Noa and Liat, husband to Michael Simon, and Lead Rabbi of Shir Tikvah Congregation in Minneapolis, Minnesota, where he has served since July 2009. He is the immediate past co-Chair of T'ruah: The Rabbinic Call for Human Rights, a Senior Rabbinic Fellow of the Shalom Hartman Institute, and was a co-instigator/found of Dreaming Up High Holy Days 5781 (now Dreaming 5781) on Facebook.*

IS IT TOO EARLY TO MAKE MEANING?

Rabbi Maura Linzer

Suddenly it's quiet. How'd that happen? No email to answer. No text message waiting for a response. No sibling fights to break up. Oh, how should I spend these precious quarantine minutes? Fold the laundry pile on my dresser that looks like the Tower of Pisa? Unload the dishwasher? Sneak a few minutes of 90 Day Fiancé? I settle on calling a friend.

By some miracle, she answers. "Wow, you're alive!" she begins. "Despite all odds," I respond. "How are *you*?" There is silence on the other end, intermittently filled with children screaming in the background. She answers, "Well *you* know."

There is so much to unpack in that silence: months filled with anxiety, pain, and loss. But I wonder if that's the whole story, the only story. What else might be buried in there? Is it too early to make meaning of the pandemic and what we've been through, if we are still living it? Are we ready to go there?

We are in month six. Usually when we're faced with stressful times, we can draw on past experience for guidance. But we've had no road map for these last six months. We're in uncharted territory.

Certain memories stand out, signposts that our reality had changed: Do you remember when many of us got up in the middle of the night to try and get a food delivery slot from Fresh Direct? Or when we searched grocery stores for one coveted six-pack of toilet paper?

IS IT TOO EARLY TO MAKE MEANING?

And when we tried to convince ourselves that the warm weather would kill the virus and our children would return to school in April or by May at the latest?

We have all made decisions and instantly second guessed them. At night, we made plans based on CDC guidelines only to wake up to brand new recommendations. One day we didn't need a mask, the next day we were urged to consider it and then almost overnight, masks were mandatory.

And as we moved forward, we didn't look back. Who had time or the energy to stop and think about the journey we were on, when we were just trying to make it through each day?

But *now* is the time to look back. Yom Kippur is a Jewish experience unlike any other. Tonight and tomorrow, we are encouraged to enter into a state of reflection, to consider our lives over the past year, all while acknowledging the uncertainty of our future. On this Yom Kippur, we have more to reflect on than perhaps any other year, and we're going to begin the process tonight, even though it might be difficult. Because this is exactly what we need.

We cannot gather in our beautiful sanctuary tonight, but we *can* enter into this sacred time of reflection together. So let us take a few moments to consider the range of experiences among our Beth El community.

Some of us who are at an increased health risk have not ventured beyond our mailboxes in six months. Others have been unable to visit our loved ones in nursing homes and care centers. Many of us have grown accustomed to working at home side by side with our spouses, without childcare, flipping pancakes while we homeschool our children and walk the new dog--all at the same time. Many are struggling financially as companies have downsized and restructured to stay afloat. Some of us have welcomed our grown children back into our homes or had other relatives come to live with us. Some of us have suffered the painful loss of loved ones during this pandemic and had to bury them without even having a chance to say goodbye. And the list goes on.

Yes, it's been bad, terrible even. But has it *all* been bad? After all, some of us now spend less time commuting to and from work and more time with our families. We have had dinner with our children every night regularly for the first time in their lives. Zoom has allowed us to connect with our loved ones near and far; and be present for moments that we might have otherwise missed. Our circumstances have born creative rituals such as car parades and drive-in graduations. We now spend more time in nature and have developed a new appreciation for our environment. We refused to let the pandemic disrupt our commitment to *Tikkun Olam*, and collected thousands of pounds of food for those in need. Our members have made hundreds of phone calls to keep us all connected. And our attendance at virtual shabbat services has increased dramatically, as we seek to connect with one another.

We also were able to launch Better Together, a program of the Legacy Heritage Foundation that paired Beth El teens with seniors for weekly virtual activities during the summer. These partnerships impacted both our teens and seniors in unexpected ways. One of our teen participants, Jordy Singer shared that little things like talking to someone new after months of isolation can make a huge difference in how she felt in her day-to-day life. Long-time congregant, Carol Saltzman, reflected that her participation in the program was a very special light in an otherwise dark period. She appreciated how energizing and fun it was to chat with her new friends, and she hopes that their relationship continues long after the program ends. These are the rare glimmers of hope that have sustained us.

According to Jewish tradition, it is not enough to offer our prayers tonight. We are also required to include *Kavanot*, our reflections and self-assessment on the year gone by.

To guide us through this process, I ask you to think about what you've overcome during the last six months and what have you learned about yourself? What did you do that you never imagined you could?

Tonight, once the service ends and you log off, I encourage you to share your thoughts. If you are alone, you might put your feelings into words, either by sharing them with a friend or perhaps writing a letter to yourself.

I can tell you; I've spent a lot of time reflecting on my own journey over the past six months. And to be honest it's been a painful and emotional road. I remember each and every challenge that I've faced. Last spring, my husband and I pulled our children out of school, because of my severe asthma. Then only days later our au pair decided that she needed to return home to Spain to help her family. Suddenly, we found ourselves homeschooling two children, one with severe learning differences, while I simultaneously tried to serve the needs of the community and while my husband worked alongside us at our kitchen table. We remember cancelling our long-awaited trip to Europe and our plans to send our children to camp. All of these decisions seemed excruciating until the phone rang late one night, and we learned that my father-in-law in Israel had passed away and we wouldn't be able to go to the funeral or even enter their home for *shiva* due to the tight quarantine orders in Israel. Suddenly, all of those previous decisions seemed trivial.

But while there have been so many difficult moments, some I didn't know how we'd make it through, we did. And tonight, I reflect on our many blessings as well. My family and I have spent so many wonderful moments together, hiking, biking, and just being a family-- moments I certainly would have otherwise missed. I've made bedtime every single night for 6 months for the first time in my life, and I've reconnected with my husband--even if there were moments we wanted to kill each other along the way. I know that none of you can possibly relate. I've also strengthened my ties to my friends, who have been there to support me and hold me up, when I didn't think I could do it myself. And I've realized just how strong I am. After these last six months, I truly believe I can overcome anything.

Tonight, I want us to celebrate our inner strength and resilience. We are here. We are a bit broken, yes, but we have persisted, adapted, and grown in ways that we never imagined.

Tonight, I challenge us to share our strength. Find those individuals who need to be lifted up. They can be a neighbor, a relative who lives alone, or a friend, who is isolated due to increased health risk. Reach out to them and connect. Let's strive for more than a text message or a quick hello. Consider what you can do to let them know you care. When you ask, "is there something you need?" many will probably say no, they don't need anything. So, come ready with ideas: Can I bring over a meal? Schedule a weekly socially distanced conversation? Help with grocery shopping? If you are told, no, you are not exempt! It might mean you need to get more creative!

Performing acts of loving-kindness remind us that we are alive. They help us remain balanced and grateful when our world feels like it's spinning out of control. On this Yom Kippur, may we rediscover the light inside of each of us and may we rekindle the spirit of those we love.

Let us acknowledge how truly grateful we are to be alive to enter into a new year together with *Shehecheyanu*. I invite you to say it with me:

IS IT TOO EARLY TO MAKE MEANING?

Baruch atah, Adonai Eloheinu, Melech haolam, shehechyanu v'kiy'manu, v'higiyanu laz'man hazeh.

Blessed are you, Adonai our God, Sovereign of the universe, who has sustained us in ways we never imagined possible, and helped us to reach this moment in time. *Shana Tova.*

Rabbi Maura Linzer *serves as the Associate Rabbi-Educator of Temple Beth El of Northern Westchester. She was ordained at the Cincinnati campus of HUC-JIR in 2012. She received an MA in Hebrew Letters from HUC-JIR in 2011 and an MA in Religious Education from the HUC-JIR in 2013. Rabbi Linzer earned an MA in Middle Eastern Studies from Ben Gurion University in 2010 and graduated with honors with a BA from Washington University in St. Louis. Rabbi Linzer received the Jewish Education Project Young Pioneer Award in 2019 for her innovative work in the field of Jewish education.*

TIKKUN, TESHUVAH, AND SELF-CARE

Rabbi Dara Lithwick

Shabbat Shalom and Shanah Tovah U'metukah!

We are at the start of a new year, a birthday of creation, a time of possibility and renewal. I want to extend a shout out to my father in Montreal who is also celebrating a special birthday today.

Happy birthday dad!

Once, when Rosh Hashanah fell on a Shabbat (like now), Hasidic 18th century Rabbi Levi Yitzchak of Berditchev declared, *"Ribono Shel Olam*, Master of the Universe, You forbid us to write on Shabbat except in order to save a life. So write us down in the Book of Life, since otherwise even You may not write on Shabbat."[18]

Hopefully this means that we are off to a promising start!

Seriously, though, a year ago who could have imagined, who would have wanted to imagine, that we would be welcoming in 5781 like this – from our homes, in our little boxes, zoomed out, trying to stay safe from COVID-19, all the while fires rage in the west and hurricanes threaten the southeast. And then there is our increased collective awareness of systemic racism and more…

---

[18] From *Sefer Hachasidut*, cited in Abraham Yaakov Finkel, *The Essence of the Holy Days*, p. 16.

TIKKUN, TESHUVAH, AND SELF-CARE

The past months have been alienating for many of us, in many different ways: some of us have been isolated, alone in our apartments, some have been struggling to juggle our kids' schooling and work and more all from the kitchen table, some of us haven't been able to see family members because of distance or risk or closed international borders.

Let's take a minute and sit with that. This, here, is really hard, on a lot of levels. It's okay to feel it, to name it. To mourn what was and what could have been in an alternate world without COVID-19. To miss being in connected, physical community.

And still, we are here, and we are together, albeit differently. We have adapted with our tradition, we have figured out new ways to stay socially connected while maintaining physical distance. We have figured out how to be holy at home. Sort of.

And while connections may drop or screens may freeze or we may lose our place, through the ether we are here and we are together.

I feel as though it isn't chance that this year, Rosh Hashanah, the new year, also coincides with Shabbat because goodness do we need some rest and some wholeness and the ability to turn the page on the year that has been!

Two interrelated themes are especially prominent throughout the High Holidays, that of **teshuvah** and of **tikkun**. I am going to unpack these throughout the next 10 days, through Yom Kippur.

TIKKUN, TESHUVAH, AND SELF-CARE

Teshuvah literally means "returning" or reconciliation, and *tikkun* means repair or healing. Our tradition teaches us that in many ways *teshuvah* is the path to *tikkun,* be it at the individual level (*tikkun atzmi*), the familial and communal level (*tikkun klali*), and for the whole world (*tikkun olam*).

We need *teshuvah* and *tikkun* more than ever now… Let's frame it this way: how to reconnect and reconcile and heal through the various forms of disconnection, alienation, isolation that have become so present in the past year – COVID-19, wildfires, racism, violence (i.e. gun violence).

When we talk about doing *teshuvah*, particularly in the context of the High Holidays, the sense is often that of seeking forgiveness for ways that we have strayed from our best selves, ways that we have unintentionally or intentionally hurt others.

More deeply, though, **teshuvah** is about re-centering ourselves, recalibrating ourselves, finding **balance** in ourselves, to be able to then heal and spread healing and repair around us.

In fact, in order to heal and repair our world, **we** need to be able to be well, safe, and fulfilled. Otherwise we burn out – alienated from ourselves **and** from the others we hope to help.

Teshuvah is **self-care**. And self-care is not selfish.

Teshuvah and tikkun start with us as individuals and expand out.

TIKKUN, TESHUVAH, AND SELF-CARE

Rav Abraham Isaac Kook, first chief rabbi of British Mandate Palestine, offered a brilliant teaching on the shofar as a model for such *teshuvah* and tikkun:[19]

Traditionally, before blowing the shofar on Rosh Hashanah, we recite the verse from Psalms: "From my **straits** I called out to God. He answered me, and set me in a **wide expanse**." (Psalms 118:5)

Imagine the narrows of the Psalm verse as the narrow, private issues of the individual, and the expanse as the broad, general concerns of the community and the world. The shofar, then, with its widening shape, is a metaphor of the widening circle/cycle of reconciliation and repair. Again, we start with ourselves, right here and right now, and from there reach out to really care for the needs of our communities and our world.

In this metaphor, we start from the self, but we are not alone. As our tradition emphasizes time and again, we are social and communal beings.

In the words of the immortal Bill Withers, *z"l*: "If there is a load, you have to bear/ That you can't carry/I'm right up the road/I'll share your load/If you just call me."

We are and will be here for you, for us, for each other.

And the "we" is intentional. It has taken a cross-continental village to make these services happen. We are bending time and space with Chazzan Daniela here live from Los Angeles. We have Paula and others leading us in song from home here in Toronto. We are

---

[19] http://www.ravkooktorah.org/ROSH_HAS58.htm

so grateful to Vered and the choir for the beautiful offerings that will unfold. Matt is producing all of this in live time, which is an unbelievable undertaking. And special thanks to Natalie, administrator extraordinaire, and particular extra special thanks to the Board and the High Holiday planning committee who have put endless hours of sweat and some tears to bring this together. We have been doing our best to reach beyond technology back into the real world, delivering messages and gift bags as tokens of our connection to each other, helping navigate technology, and enabling us to share in community together one way or another.

We all need somebody to lean on, now more than ever. I am grateful that we have each other.

Finally, last week's Torah portion, *Nitzavim*, which is always the Torah portion that precedes Rosh Hashanah, (and spoiler alert, we'll come back to at Yom Kippur), contains a core message of Jewish tradition, faith, and agency: We read (Deut. 30:19): "I call heaven and earth to witness you today: I have put before you life and death, blessing and curse — therefore choose life!"

There is a beautiful challenge in choosing life – it's on us. *Aleinu.* We are called on to **cultivate resiliency**, to take the small baby steps of life we can choose every day, to be grateful, to breathe, to take care of ourselves and each other, to advocate, to march for justice, to gather safely in community, to get some sleep. This time of year especially, our tradition gives us a toolkit through *teshuvah* **and** *tikkun* to choose life, to literally **inscribe** *ourselves* **in the book of life and blessing.** May

115

we all do so, and lean on each other as much as we can to get there.

Shana Tovah U'metukah.

Rabbi Dara Lithwick *is passionate about building bridges between people and communities and promoting inclusion as a fundamental Jewish practice. She is an advocate for LGBTQ2+ inclusion within diverse Jewish spaces, as well as for Jewish inclusion in LGBTQ2+ spaces. When not at work as a constitutional and parliamentary affairs lawyer, Rabbi Lithwick is active as an outreach rabbi at Temple Israel Ottawa, where she helps lead services and lifecycle events, teach adult and youth programs, and engage in outreach and social action initiatives, and led High Holiday services at Congregation Shir Libeynu in Toronto, the longest standing LGBTQ-inclusive shul in the city. Rabbi Lithwick is also chairing a Canadian Council for Reform Judaism group to develop a Tikkun Olam strategy for Canada and is the Canadian representative to the Union for Reform Judaism's Commission on Social Action. She also serves on the JSpace Canada Advisory Board, and on the LGBTQ2+ Advisory Council at CIJA, the Centre for Israel and Jewish Affairs. Rabbi Lithwick and her partner love chasing their two children around Ottawa.*

FINDING OUR WAY OUT TOGETHER

Rabbi Yael Ridberg

A parable of Rabbi Hayyim of Zans: A sojourner had been wandering about in a forest for several days, not knowing which was the right way out. Suddenly he saw someone approaching him. His heart filled with anticipation. "Now I will learn which is the right way," he thought. When they neared one another, he asked: "Please tell me which is the right way out of this forest. I have been wandering about for several days." Said the other to him, "I do not know the way out either, for I too have been wandering about here for many, many, days. But this I can tell you: do not take the way I have been going, for that will lead you astray. Now let us look for a new way together."

I used to see this reading as a metaphor for the work of *teshuvah* that we each must do ourselves, but that having a companion along can help us feel less alone. I was always the "someone" in the tale, coming to support and help others find their way out. This year, I see it very differently, for I am the sojourner wandering about in a forest lost and unsure of the path. I thought I knew where to go, and what to do. But the truth of the last months for me is I have been putting off loss and grief, sadness and paralysis, because I didn't want to feel the pain that I knew lived beneath the surface, potentially crowding out my "can do" attitude, my "Messiah complex" and my desire to help others before myself.

I knew a time would come when I would need to feel it all. I just wasn't prepared for it to be today. But we plan and God laughs. I'm quite sure God's been hysterical for six months.

The beginning of the quarantine came with productivity and positivity along with masks and limited visits to the grocery store. We stocked up our pantry, we made learning spaces for the kids, we cancelled vacations, and wiped down our grocery bags.

But with the passing of days into weeks, the minutes were full but the hours empty. Rushing was replaced with paralysis. My children may or may not have watched Netflix for 8 hours on any given day. I myself may have managed to get through 4/7 seasons of The West Wing since March. There were infinite moments of stress and yelling by everyone in my house. More than once. Too much time isolated from friends and work, too much time together in one place. And when the days got longer, time seemed without end.

I thought about that moment when Moses came down the mountain carrying the Ten Commandments and saw the people dancing and worshipping a golden calf. The text says, *"Vayihar aff Moshe"*–Moses became enraged and hurled the tablets from his hands and shattered them.[20]

---

[20] Exodus 32:19

The interpretation I had always understood was simply that Moses was angry and frustrated. But I read a midrash recently that completely altered my understanding. The rabbis explain that the letters of the words inscribed on the tablets were what made it possible for Moses to carry them down the mountain. The Divine instructions themselves lightened Moses' load, because they were aspirational and instructional. The words said everything a newly free people needed to know to make their way in the world.

But in the moment when Moses saw the people with the calf, exhibiting a loss of faith and certainty, the letters of the commandments flew off the tablets causing them to be suddenly unbearably heavy, and Moses didn't have the strength to hold them, so they fell to the ground, and shattered.[21]

Moses received a second set of tablets, we know, but the broken segments of the first set were not discarded. They were placed in the *aron* – the ark that travelled with the Israelites while in the wilderness.[22] The word for the tablets used in the text is *edut* – the same word for bearing witness. The broken Tablets were a way to remember that which Moses witnessed, even if it was shattering. And they likely were a way for the people to remember what can happen in isolation, and how uncertainty and anxiety, are very much a part of life.

---

[21] Midrash Tanhuma, Ki Tissa 30
[22] Talmud Bava Batra 14b

We might also remember that the Ten Commandments deal with the human-Divine and human-human relationships and are meant to lighten the load of what it means to be a human being in the world. Over the last 6 months in isolation, uncertainty, and anxiety, I collected the unbearable broken pieces of life, and they have been stored in my holy of holies, but I never really paid them much mind. Until this past week when a morning routine went south, the kids were late, voices were raised, and when they left, I dissolved in a puddle of tears weeping over everything from the mundane to the catastrophic.

When I told a friend about my morning, she said: "Meltdowns are so important. I'm probably due for one soon too."

"Al eileh ani bochiya," for these things do I weep, my eyes flow tears" says the author of Lamentations (1:16) in response to the destruction of Jerusalem. If I could have conducted Yom Kippur from that moment of release, I would have.

The collective trauma of the last year cannot be underestimated. Dr. Molly Casteloe, an expert in group psychology defines this kind of trauma as: a shared experience of helplessness, disorientation, and loss among a group of people… when "the threatening event gives rise to a shared identification — despite the fact that the victimized individuals have different personalities and family backgrounds, different coping mechanisms and capacities for resilience."[23]

This is a public health catastrophe, a failure of democracy and its ideals," she explains. "The deaths of so many — the elderly, the infirm, local healthcare workers and first responders — is already everyday a shared trauma among us."

We have been sustaining a level of anxiety and loss without an obvious end in sight, and it has been taxing on even the strongest of heart. And let's be clear, there can be no normalization of this tragedy and trauma. There is no, "It is what it is."

There are more 200,000 dead in the US, 1 million dead worldwide; The healthcare system has been overwhelmed; Mask wearing and social distancing have been politicized; The terrifying domino effect of economic chaos in our country and around the world, with increasing numbers of people unemployed, homeless and uninsured, has been devastating; and the fact is that COVID-19 has not been a great equalizer: its impact particularly devastating for communities of color, the poor and too many other disenfranchised communities in our midst, makes it worse.

The ongoing experience of COVID-19 is the foundation of trauma we have experienced this year, but it is only

---

[23] https://www.rollingstone.com/culture/culture-features/covid-19-coronavirus-collective-trauma-memorial monument-history-994173/

the first layer of compounding losses. The second layer is that we find ourselves in the deeply overdue reckoning on racism and police brutality, which belies the 400 year-old collective trauma of slavery. In the last 6 months we have witnessed the killing of black men and women killed or shot at while living their lives. We say their names: Ahmed Aubrey, Breonna Taylor, George Floyd and Jacob Blake. I am sickened when I think about it.

When I consider the Jewish collective trauma of anti-Semitism in America that still lives and breathes two years after the Tree of Life Massacre and the shooting in Poway, I feel the anxiety rise as well. The horrific attacks at the Jersey City Kosher Supermarket and the one on Chanukah in Monsey NY are just two brutal examples. In addition, the pushing out of Jewish activists in progressive spaces whether in city government or the ivory tower of academia, because of the complexity of Israel-Palestine conflict is worrisome at best.

For most of us this is the first time in our lifetime that doubling and tripling of efforts and time will not result in a work product that reflects the effort. And that's because there is a current reality beyond our control. Like other traumas involving loss, the limitations of the pandemic grip are encountered anew, every time we have tried to do something we used to be able to do thoughtlessly. And each time we are introduced to the loss all over again.

We have grown to expect to want the best, do our best and have the best. But the more effort we put in the more mediocre the results sometimes feel. We have never encountered such a pervasive and persistent disabler in our lives. It's been humbling. There are no ideal scenarios, only the best we can do.

This became obvious to me as lost sacred time markers and rituals became the third layer of disorientation and displacement. As a parent of a member of the now infamous Class of 2020, I received her teary phone call on March 12 that school was over, her senior year irrevocably altered. "It's not fair" she cried. "I know," I said. And then I cried.

My family wasn't alone of course. The graduations, the *bnai mitzvah*, the weddings, the funerals all experienced in ways one of us would have wanted. The adjustments, the alterations, the cancellations became dominos of loss and grief. But my job was to say, "It would all be ok. We'll make it work." So we dressed up to watch the graduation on line, my daughter moved the tassel on her cap as we stood in our living room and we toasted her achievement.

I performed *b'nai mitzvah* in backyards, listening to grandparents recite the Torah blessings in delayed cacophony. I offered comfort in zoom shiva minyanim without hugs, but with multiple screens showing family and friends from all over the country.

After RH services I actually worried that when the time comes to resume some sense of pre-COVID normalcy, I won't remember how to do it.

These multilayered experiences of trauma and loss are all around us, and the grief we share is a profound expression of love for one another, our country, and the world. And we also know, at least existentially, that we are not he first to suffer. After the destruction of the Second temple in Jerusalem our ancestors replaced sacrifices with study, prayer, and acts of loving kindness; after the Holocaust, Jewish families resurrected life in the second, third, and now fourth generation with creativity, brilliance, agitation, and a profound sense of urgency to re-build out of the ashes.

In one of my favorite interpretations of Psalm 23, Rabbi Harold Kushner teaches that the most powerful action verse is: *Gam ki elech b'gei tzalmavet – lo ira ra – ki atah imadi.* "Yay though I walk through the valley of death, I will not be afraid, For You are with me God." Kushner teaches that it is no mistake that the verse says "though I walk through" the valley of death. For it might well have been rendered, "though I get stuck in the valley of death," but it doesn't. God isn't there to prevent, protect, or to justify the challenges humanity will ultimately face; rather, God is there for comfort and strength, when we are in the midst of such challenges.

"The human soul is capable of astonishing resilience. Don't be afraid of the future, not because life will be without suffering, or that good people will always get what they deserve, but because good people in difficult circumstances can come up with the spiritual and emotional resources to deal with what comes."[24]

Trauma, suffering, and loss are valleys we walk through to something on the other side that we don't yet know. Yet we are not alone. We must grieve the losses of this past year, the personal, the communal, and the global. Each of us has likely travelled the spiral staircase of grief like that Escher drawing where you cannot tell if the stairs are going up or down, and where they lead.

Kubler Ross' stages of grief: Denial – anger – bargaining – depression – acceptance are not linear, in my experience, nor is there a single moment when grief is "over." But Viktor Frankl's *Man's Search for Meaning* reminds us that the will to move through a valley of dark shadows depends on seeing life as a quest for meaning. "We must retain the ability to choose our attitude; We must realize there will be suffering and it's how we react to suffering that counts; There is power in purpose; The true test of character is in how we act; And human kindness can be found in the most surprising places."[25]

These sentiments, while written in 1945 after Frankl survived the Holocaust, were embodied by two

---

[24] https://www.pbs.org/wnet/religionandethics/2004/11/26/november-26-2004-harold-kushner/15271/

[25] https://www.realtimeperformance.com/5-lessons-from-viktor-frankls-book-mans-search-for-meaning/

American heroes whom we lost this year: Rep. John Lewis who died in July, and Justice Ruth Bader Ginsburg who died last week.

They were of the same generation, from completely different backgrounds, but each was an ordinary person who saw the ways society was lost, and became legendary American warriors for justice and equity, compassion and empathy to build an America where "we the people" could be expanded exponentially to include everyone.

Both of them endured discrimination, loss, and trauma, and went on to live lives of meaning that made it possible for others to do so as well. Their loss is profound, and we might wonder who will fill their shoes? But each of them was like the person in the parable who said to the lost sojourner: "Let's find a new way out together."

In his letter to America shared after his death John Lewis wrote: "You must also study and learn the lessons of history because humanity has been involved in this soul-wrenching, existential struggle for a very long time. People on every continent have stood in your shoes, though decades and centuries before you. The truth does not change, and that is why the answers worked out long ago can help you find solutions to the challenges of our time...Though I may not be here with you, I urge you to answer the highest calling of your heart and stand up for what you truly believe. ...let the spirit of peace and the power of everlasting love be your guide."[26]

And just this week, my friend and colleague, Rabbi Lauren Holtzblatt, eulogizing the Justice reflected: "To be born into a world that doesn't see you, that does not believe in your potential, that does not give you a path for opportunity, or education, and despite this, to be able to see beyond the world you are in, to imagine that something can be different. That is the job of a prophet. And it is the rare prophet who not only imagines a new world, but also makes that new world a reality, in her lifetime."[27]

When a person dies, we say *zikhronam livrakha* – "may their memory be a blessing." We turn the memories of those we loved and admired, whether we knew them or not, into blessings, and the example of their lives into an ever-expanding view of the world and its challenges.

Today on Yom Kippur, we recognize our own mortality, and all that have sacrificed these past 6 months. Let us grieve and weep for what we have lost, show up for those who need it most, and let us re-build the world we

---

[26] https://www.nytimes.com/2020/07/30/opinion/john-lewis-civil-rights-america.html
[27] www.nytimes.com/video/us/politics/100000007356706/justice-ginsburg-rabbi-eulogy.html

know is possible with the sacred values and vision that will help lighten the load we carry every day.

May goodness and steadfast love pursue us all the days of our life, and may we come to dwell in divine wholeness and holiness for our length of days.

Gmar Hatima Tovah – May we find our way out, together.

Rabbi Yael B. Ridberg *has served as the rabbi of Congregation Dor Hadash in San Diego, California since 2010. She is the Past-President of the San Diego Jewish Academy Board of Trustees. She is also a Past-President of the Reconstructionist Rabbinical Association and previously served on the Board of Jewish Family Service of San Diego. Rabbi Ridberg's writing has appeared in Times of Israel, Huffington Post, and Kveller. A transplanted New Yorker, she lives in La Jolla with her husband and four daughters.*

PRAYING TOGETHER, YET APART

Rabbi Adrienne Rubin

Many people spend more hours in shul over High Holy Days than the rest of the year combined. They come to services even if they don't find them enriching and fulfilling, because it's our tradition and what we have always done. This year is different. No one is looking to see whether we are there and what we are doing or what we ae wearing. This year, since you are here, watching and listening now, I hope it is not because you are under duress, or feel obligation or guilt. This year is your opportunity to make the service and the prayers your own.

We have been saying these prayers for a long, long time. They began to be institutionalized around the time of the Babylonian exile, when the rabbis were concerned about the dilution of prayer in the absence of Temple sacrifices. At first, our ancestors recited all of our prayers by heart. That is a lot of words, isn't it? After a while, just like a game of telephone, the set prayers being passed from one person to another risked being changed, so their words were written down. By the Middle Ages, the texts of the prayers were nearly fixed. We have been saying the same words every year in each generation for hundreds of years, connecting to the history and longevity of these words and our people is one way we can make these prayers our own.

We may know the liturgy from years of having heard it, but how well do we really know it? How do we connect to it? How do we draw meaning from it? Unless one is fluent in Hebrew, it is probably through the translations. This can present a challenge! Frequently, the English translations can feel awkward, old, stilted, unreal. And the imagery can make us uncomfortable. Our machzor – *Machzor Chadash* – the new *Machzor* – was written and published in 1977. It's not so new anymore and the language reflects that.

In any translation, it is hard to capture the essence, the nuance of the original language and Hebrew to English is no exception. Take *Sh'ma*, for example. It can mean "hear" or "listen". Which is correct? Well, both. Which is better? Well, that depends, doesn't it? And *Echad* can mean "one" and also "alone". Some prayer books have one and some have the other. Which is better? That's up to you to decide. It is hard work to be a translator. The words they choose can change the prayer's interpretation and can impact the way we connect to it.

Luckily, we don't need to use the literal translations to find meaning in the prayers; we can explore the concept of a prayer or part of a prayer. For example, a challenging prayer any year, but especially this year, is *Unetaneh Tokef* – who shall live and who shall die. Do we really want to take these words literally? That it is predetermined which of us will live and die in the coming year and how? Or do we want to focus on the last line – that *t'shuvah*, *t'filah* and *tz'dakah*, repentance, prayer and righteousness or charity, can lessen the decree given us. For me, that line helps me focus on how I want to live my life. Connecting to the purpose of particular prayers and creating our own personal interpretations of them is another way we can make these prayers our own.

We are not restricted by the prayers in the Machzor. After all, Judaism has a long history of personal prayer. The Torah is full of these "conversations with God." Abraham, Issac and Jacob, Moses… they all pray to God. Personal prayer is steeped in our history and stories. For me, personal prayer is my opportunity to bring voice to my deepest longings, my need for strength, my joy and my sadness. It helps me begin journeys with confidence and strength and end them with acceptance and completion. Finding our inner voices, that connection with our true selves is another way we can make these prayers our own.

Our rabbis knew that personal prayer in community with others deepens each of our journeys. Our confessional is in the plural. WE have sinned. WE have missed the mark. When we read the *Al Cheit*, when we sing *Ashamnu*, we connect to the self-reflection of the person next to us. We learn from their lessons and they learn from ours. And somehow, going through this together makes the process less onerous.

Our Talmud teaches that if two people enter to pray, and one of them finishes praying first and doesn't wait for their fellow and leaves, their prayer is torn up in their face (*B'rachot* 5b). But if the first person to finish waits, they will receive rich rewards, including peace and the legacy of children and family. In other words, when we bear witness to the value of someone else's prayer, such as when we wait until the last person has finished the Amidah, our own prayers are magnified. If we act as if only our own prayers are important, they are nullified.

How do we do this this year? We are doing it right now. We cannot see each other on YouTube, but we are here with each other nonetheless. Just look at how many people are watching this! When our congregants came to record Torah and prayers, they were preparing to stand with each of us as we pray in these moments. Supporting each other to pray, even when we cannot see each other or be together in person, is another way we can make these prayers our own.

Finally, a way many of us pray is through music. Rabbi Eddie Feld, my college Rabbi and the editor of the Conservative Movement's, *Lev Shalem Siddur* and *Machzor*, had a sign on his wall I have never forgotten: "They who sing pray twice." The High Holy Day music contains melodies we only hear at this time of year. And no words are needed for them to be powerful. If I sing <*Ashamnu* chorus> you know exactly what it is – *Ashamnu*, our group confessionals. If I sing <*Avinu Malkeinu*>, you know it is *Avinu Malkeinu* – Our Father, Our King (or Our Parent Our Sovereign if that speaks more to you!) These melodies allow our hearts to pray.

And whether we sing along or just listen to the melodies washing over us, this is perhaps the easiest, and for some the most meaningful, way we can make these prayers our own.

This day is about you and your journey, past, present and future. My wish for you is that you find the deepest, most personal connection to your prayers. If you are fasting, may your fasting intensify your prayers. If you are not fasting, may your observance of *pikuach nefesh* do the same. Whether through Hebrew or English, personal or communal, spoken or sung, may you make these prayers your own so that your Yom Kippur in this very different year gives you exactly what you need.

G'mar Chatimah Tovah.

Rabbi Adrienne Rubin *has been bringing meaning into people's lives at synagogues for over 30 years. She is the Rabbi at Temple Beth Ahm Yisrael, a Conservative Synagogue in Springfield, NJ. Prior to this, she served as Cantorial Soloist at Temple Micah, an unaffiliated, egalitarian synagogue in Lawrenceville, NJ, for 24 years, as the High Holy Day Cantor for the University of Rhode Island for five years, and as a guest cantor and soloist for several synagogues in Massachusetts. Rabbi Rubin graduated from Princeton University in 1988 with a B.A. in Music Theory and Composition and she is a trained opera singer. She received S'micha from the Rabbinical Seminary International and is a member of the International Federation of Rabbis, Rabbinical Fellowship of America, the Women Cantors' Network, 18Doors (formerly Interfaith Family Network), Equally Wed and the Rainbow Wedding Network. Rabbi Rubin lives in Princeton, NJ, with her husband Doug and their son, Elian, who is a student at Oberlin College.*

RACISM AND JUDAISM

Rabbi Cantor Robbi Sherwin

Shalom, y'all!

With the nation on fire – literally and figuratively, we are finally having the very hard conversations – some in the media and some in the streets - about the systemic racial injustice that has been suffered by people of color in the United States. But, what is happening in our own Jewish communities? Jews of color, make up approximately 12-15% of the Jewish population in the US.[28] They consist of interracial groupings that come with a very different Jewish background or world view, but although it has been proven that we Jews are not a RACE – the acceptance of Jews of color even among us– the Jews–you know, the cultural/religious/historically scapegoated People of the Book? has been iffy at best.

Even though we, as Jews, don't consider ourselves "racist" in the traditional sense – after all, aren't we one of the most persecuted people throughout history? systemic Jewish racism exists within our own ranks. Many of my colleagues who are Jews of color often get asked when they converted. Or what they are doing in synagogue. Or why they even want to be Jewish. Or if they were adopted. Numerous articles have been written about how unwelcome Jews of color feel among our ranks and I have heard quite a few pod casts on this

---

[28] eJewishPhilanthropy.com, May 17, 2020

subject, as well. You may have heard that the newest Disney Princess is a Latinx Jew? It's a start.

I have a colleague from rabbinical school, Abshalom, now living in the Amish country of Pennsylvania, and whose family came from Barbados to the US generations ago via Ethiopia. He is from the Ethiopian Jewish clan known as Beta Israel, the House of Israel, which can be traced back to the tribe of Dan. Wow - these Jews can trace their lineage for thousands of years and most of us can't trace much farther back than the Warsaw Ghetto. But, even though we are both American Jews, our cultural divides could fill a canyon. My cultural history is informed like that of a typical Ashkenzai Jew: my family comes from Poland, Romania, and Ukraine. My Jewish cultural roots are the Borscht Belt/Dirty Dancing/Marvelous Mrs. Maisel/Mazel ball soup/half-sour pickle culture that many of us Ashkenazi Jews relate to. His cultural history is informed by Martin Luther King and Malcolm X and the Civil rights movement. When Abshalom preaches – and I mean PREACHES his *d'vrei torah* or sermons, he sounds like the minsters of the 60's. He preaches with PASSion, with conVICtion with a certain CAdence in his voice. He calls God "The Most High." He keeps strictly Kosher and even slaughters a whole lamb for the Pesach sacrifice at Passover. No one falls asleep during his sermons. He is, by far, much more observant than I am.

Abshalom is also a Jewish educator, a phlebotomist, a body builder and wears his hair in long dreadlocks. He always wears a kippah and a *talit katan* – a prayer shawl worn under clothing with the Tzitzit – the fringes - on the outside. Did I mention that he was more observant that I am?

When we were in Rabbinical school, he would head home after teaching at the Ethiopian Jewish Beta Israel Shul, to Janet, his beautiful wife, and his surviving child, his son, Shamayah. They had a daughter, Shira, which is also my Hebrew name, who died at age 8 of sickle cell anemia. Sickle cell anemia is not a known "Jewish" disease. Abshalom's family is not prone to a "Jewish" disease, Taysachs, as they are not Eastern European/Ashkenazi Jews.

So, in heading home from shul - Abshalom, this beloved teacher, scholar and rabbi - quite often couldn't get a cab to stop for him in Brooklyn – because he is BLACK. Let that sink in for a moment.

I am Jewish. I consider myself and my people a persecuted minority. But, unless I am wearing a kippah or some outward, recognized symbol of Judaism, I pass for merely white.

Robin DiAngelo, Author of the riveting and startling book, "White Fragility," was in Sun Valley a couple of summers ago. In her 3-hour workshop, I was SHOCKED to discover some of the ways that I myself was racist. I would hold very tight to my purse if there were black kids walking next to me on the sidewalk; I heard my grandparents, who owned a big bakery/catering operation in Cleveland call their help (forgive me) "shvartzes," a pejorative term for Black people. As for me, and as for most of us, the only black teachers I had growing up were PE teachers or coaches.

Abshalom joined me for the high Holidays in my former pulpit in Crested Butte, CO about 6 years ago. And, as we learned a lot from this scholar and mensch – he took us WAY out of our comfort zones.

He and I sat down and had a "come to Moses" talk when we were studying one day. I insisted that I totally GOT his life as a Black Jew - because my life, as a Jew, was also hard and fraught with prejudice leveled at me and my family.

"But," I protested, "I grew up in the Air Force and I had friends that were from all races. One of my best friends in my Sacramento high school, Sandy Moore, was BLACK. I'm Jewish. I was Jewish in the Air Force. I had my house vandalized repeatedly when I was a kid because we were Jewish." I whined: "My siblings and I were beaten up and bullied at school because we were Jewish."

I went on to list all the ways that I was DIFFERENT and special and also discriminated against. We all find ways to express that we are not racist – listing our qualifications as proof that we are not one of "them." From Abshalom and from Robin DiAngelo, author of White Fragility, I learned that listing all the ways that you were not racist was... racist.

"Sorry, my holy sister, "Abshalom finally sighed: "You are still white. You can drive away and still be white. You can leave everything behind, start a new life and you will STILL. BE. WHITE. I can never outrun my blackness."

Talking about our own prejudices – having these uncomfortable conversations and taking things out of our comfort zones - are the whole reason behind Rosh Hashana, Yom Kippur and the 10 days of repentance. The Talmud (*Shevuot* 39a), in discussing the domino effect of sin, concludes with the Aramaic phrase, *Kol yisrael arevim zeh bazeh*, meaning "all of Israel are responsible for each other." It's the Talmudic version of "If you see something, DO something." We must not stand idly by while our brothers and sisters of color remain continually and systematically The Other. And shame on us for fomenting this amongst ourselves. We can and we will do better.

May 5781 finally be the year that we wake up, recognize our own prejudices and truly be God's partner in making this a better world.

Shana Tovah u'metukah – may it be a good and sweet year for all.

"Rockin" Rabbi-Cantor Robbi Sherwin *("R3 'Cubed'")*
*is an energetic Rabbi & Artist-in-Residence, specializing in
Jewish retreats and congregational songwriting. She bringing
an infectious love of Judaism to all — babies to Bubbies! An
award-winning, multi-published composer of 100+ Jewish
songs, Robbi tours with her folk-rock band, Sababa! with
Steve Brodsky and Scott Leader, and has recorded 5 CDs of
original Jewish music. Her "spirited Jewish song crafting" is
sung, recorded and performed from Tulsa to Tel Aviv, Seattle
to Sydney. As past President of Women Cantors' Network,
she has been in the forefront of Jewish female recording artists;
is prominently featured on Jewish Rock Radio; and enjoys
mentoring emerging artists. A smitten mountain Rabbi, she
enjoys the "Rocky Mountain chai life" with an attitude of
high-altitude gratitude. Robbi serves the Wood River Jewish
Community in Ketchum/Sun Valley, Idaho.*

YOU DON'T HAVE TO BE A RABBI TO BE A JEW

Rabbi Dr. Oren Steinitz

With the past six months so full of tragedy, anxiety, and dread, it is hard to reflect and remember anything that happened in the year 5780 before the arrival of COVID19 turned our lives upside down. Do any of us remember the Monsey shooting during Hanukah? The Persian Gulf crisis in January that almost escalated into a Third World War? The Middle East Peace Plan that was announced in early 2020? They all seem like a vague, distant memory right now.

Among these soon-forgotten events was the death of Jewish actor and philanthropist, Kirk Douglas this past February. True, the death of a 104-year-old man, who lived a full, productive life is hardly a tragedy, and not something we would spend a lot of time contemplating while we are all surrounded by senseless deaths. To be honest, not being a movie buff myself, I am not even sure I can name one film he starred in or directed. And yet, a quote from an interview with Douglas that I only heard after his passing, has stayed with me ever since.

In a 2008 talk with Rabbi David Wolpe, who was Douglas' Torah study partner for 25 years, Douglas recalled that when he was a young boy, he particularly excelled in his synagogue's Hebrew school, and after his Bar Mitzvah the congregation offered his family to pay for his Yeshiva studies in hope that he would become a rabbi. Douglas freaked out. "It scared the hell out of me," he recalled, "because I didn't want to become a rabbi. I wanted to be an actor!"

Douglas refused the generous offer, and for a very long time drifted away from Judaism. "I grew up, went to college," he said, "but my Judaism stayed stuck in a 14-year-old boy's Hebrew schoolbook." Only much later in life he came to the conclusion that while very few of us make decisions about our adult lives based on what we knew when we were teenagers, religion seems to be an exception to the rule. Even though most of us choose our career path regardless of whether we wanted to be major league baseball players or famous musicians when we were twelve, a surprising number of people are happy to reject religion altogether based on what they learned in Hebrew School. "It took me a long time," Douglas said, "to learn that you don't have to be a rabbi [in order] to be a Jew."

The statement seems funny at first. Maybe even ridiculous. Haven't we been told again and again that being Jewish is not something you can just stop doing? That anyone born a Jew, or who chose Judaism later in life, will die a Jew, regardless of how many bacon cheeseburgers they eat? I have often said that Judaism is the Hotel California of world religions – you can check out any time you like, but you can never leave. However, if what Douglas meant is that you do not have to be a rabbi to be a *serious* Jew, then the statement is much more important than it may appear at a first glance.

The American Jewish community is full of proud Jews, and even engaged Jews. Maybe even religious Jews. A serious Jew, however, is something else entirely. Rabbi Harold Kushner famously wrote that:

> Serious Jews try [...] to bring holiness into
> their lives by sanctifying their everyday
> activities. They try to pattern their lives
> on the insights of Judaism, whether in a
> Reform, Conservative or Orthodox
> idiom, To the non-serious Jew it does not
> matter what style of synagogue service
> he stays home from, or which definition
> of *mitzvah* he ignores in his daily practice.

I would add to Rabbi Kushner's definition an
observation by the late Rabbi Neil Gillman: Judaism has
three H's – Head, Heart and Hand. Head – the serious
study of Torah, and all other Jewish texts that flow from
it; Heart – spiritual life, activated by worship, ritual and
prayer; and Hand – activism, through ethics, acts of
kindness, and social action. "Every Jew," said Rabbi
Gillman, can major in one H; minor in a second H; and
will probably not get to the third H." Nevertheless, a
serious Jew must at least know what the H's stand for
and make a serious commitment to at least one of them.

The fact of the matter is that liberal Jewish communities
often see the rabbinate as the only option for a young
person who wishes to take Judaism's first two H's –
Head and Heart – seriously. Let us be honest about this;
outside the large metropolitan areas of New York City,
Washington DC, Chicago and Los Angeles, the sight of
a young person regularly showing up at services is so
rare, so disorienting, that they are quickly assumed to
be aspiring rabbinical students. I will never forget our
first Shabbat in Calgary, when we showed up at Friday
Night services in a large Conservative synagogue. The
average age of the dozen or so elderly gentlemen who

were seated in "their seats" in the small chapel was well over seventy, and the sight of a couple in their late twenties showing up at shul was clearly something they considered out of the ordinary. They gave us a puzzled look, quickly asked if we needed to say Kaddish, and when we said no, went on to ignore us for the rest of the twelve-minute service. Over the years they got used to us, not before they started calling me 'rabbi' and recruited me to teach Junior Congregation. Do we really find serious Jewish practice so unappealing, that when we see someone drawn to it, we must assume that it has to be a career choice?

Paul Solyn once told me that as far as Hebrew School students go, the rabbi can never be a role model for Jewish practice. "Remember, it does not count if *you* take your Judaism seriously," he explained, "it is your *job*." Without a significant number of "normal people" – people like their parents, siblings and cousins – who are deeply invested in Judaism, children will not see Judaism as anything to be taken seriously. A teacher in our Sunday school once told me that a student refused to believe that Hebrew was actually a spoken language. As far as this little girl (a smart, very capable student, by the way), Hebrew was nothing but a collection of magical spells and incantations, and she could not fathom why her parents insisted in wasting her time by forcing her to engage in an something so incredibly useless. Something they themselves obviously had no interest in.

The consequences of this attitude, in my opinion, are disastrous for the survival of non-Orthodox Judaism. A religious community cannot possibly survive if it is observed solely by clergy. If the only people in a given congregation who are invested in Jewish observance and – perhaps more importantly – *serious Jewish study* are the rabbi, cantor and one or two loveable misfits, Judaism will quickly be reduced to no more than a spectator sport. Yes, I am painfully aware of the irony of using this analogy while you are watching me on a TV, computer or mobile device…

As different Jewish community leaders started planning what these High Holy Days are going to look like – and by the way, we started even earlier than you think we did – a significant number of voices from the Right end of the Conservative movement, those who wished to keep avoiding the use of technology on Shabbat and Yom Tov, suggested that instead of conducting services in packed synagogues, we divide our congregants into groups of ten or twenty, who would hold small, outdoor services by themselves. Surely, they said, there must be enough people in every congregation who can lead the prayers, blow shofar, and chant Torah. This was a sobering moment for those of us on the Left, when we tried to explain to them that in communities like ours, the reality is so different.

I get it. I really do. As the fictional Rabbi Jacob Schramm said, "Jews want their Rabbi to be the kind of Jew they don't have time to be." We all lead busy lives, we all have hundreds of other concerns, and not everyone can be "into" Judaism in that way. However, if you suddenly had the time, perhaps six months of forced quarantine, would you even know what kind of Jewish content you could fill it with?

If the last six months taught us anything, it is that Jewish life that is centered around a large building, occasional gatherings, and two or three Jewish professionals who "do Jewish" on the community's behalf, will no longer work. We spent decades pouring money into expensive buildings that overnight became unusable. Within days, it became clear that the world as we knew it will never be the same, and the Jewish world is no different. All of a sudden, two or three generations of Jews that got used to a Judaism that happens only in a building, and only with the precise directives of a Rabbi, were robbed of their Jewish identity.

We are still in the Wilderness. Still trying to make sense of a new world that makes no sense at all. The High Holy Days are traditionally a time of *heshbon nefesh* – spiritual stock-taking, and this is especially true this year. Judaism has survived bigger crises than COVID, but that was because throughout all our trials and tribulations, our people knew that even when everything else made no sense, Judaism remained a constant anchor in their lives. They relied on Rabbis and scholars for the tough questions, but their daily routine was saturated with Judaism, wherever they lived, and regardless of whether it was safe to practice publicly. Judaism was a way of life, not a set of specialty skills better left to professionals. They remembered *Parashat Nitzavim*, that we read last week; a *parasha* that promises us that

> Surely, this Instruction which I enjoin upon you this day is not too baffling for you, nor is it beyond reach. It is not in the heavens לא בשמיים היא! [...] Neither is it beyond the sea, that you should say, 'Who among us can cross to the other side of the sea and get it for us and impart it to us, that we may observe it?' No, the thing is very close to you, in your [head] and in your heart, to observe it.

Simply put – they all knew that you don't have to be a Rabbi to be a Jew.

Shannah Tovah.

Rabbi Oren Z. Steinitz *serves as the rabbi of Congregation Kol Ami in Elmira, NY, and as an adjunct professor of rabbinics in the ALEPH Ordinations Program. One of a handful of Jewish Renewal rabbis to have received s'micha as Dayan (adjudicator of Jewish Law) from ALEPH Canada's Institute of Integral Halacha, he completed his PhD in Religious Studies and Communications from the University of Calgary in 2014. His research interests include Jewish-Muslim relations, fundamentalism, conversions to Judaism and Jewish divorce (gittin). Rabbi Oren lives with his wife Adar and two energetic kids in Elmira, NY.*

THERE'S ALWAYS A RAM IN THE THICKET

Rabbi Debi Wechsler

There are years that ask questions and years that answer. (Zora Neale Hurston, Their Eyes Were Watching God) You might think that this has been a year that asked questions, and indeed it did ask many questions.

Some were trivial - Where do I buy toilet paper? Can I substitute rapid rise yeast for instant? Do I have to wipe down my groceries? Why is sixth grade math so weird now? Does this mask make my face look fat? How many people are in line at Trader Joe's?

Many were profound - How can I stay safe? What am I, if I'm not my job? Is this cough just a cough? How do I live alone - never seeing, never touching another person? When will life go back to the way it was? Are my kids falling hopelessly behind in school? Will I ever get to hug my grandchildren?

These questions, and so many more, have been our own personal wilderness, a place of wandering and fear, a place of dangers and extremes. Every single High Holy Day Torah reading, both days of Rosh Hashanah and Yom Kippur morning, takes place at least partly in a wilderness - which in biblical parlance is a place where people are tested. Abraham is tested there. Sarah is tested there. Ishamel and Isaac are tested there. Aaron the High Priest is tested there. Each asks and is asked questions.

THERE'S ALWAYS A RAM IN THE THICKET

This morning we read the story of the binding of Isaac, a narrative in which Abraham and Isaac not only walk through a wilderness, but once they reach their destination of Mount Moriah, find another type of wildness, this time a thicket, so full of trees and low brush that every creature both human and animal becomes entangled there. It's a good story to read this year after months of wandering in the wilderness expecting to imminently emerge, only to find ourselves facing a different thicket. The questions have changed, but they persist.

We all know this story. Abraham raises his arm with the knife high above the body of his beloved son Isaac to sacrifice him to God and at the last moment is stopped by an angel who calls out to him. Imagine that moment when everything that Abraham had been expecting and planning for fell apart, what was he to do? What do any of us do when our reality changes so drastically?

One of the hardest things when a marriage ends, or when a couple can't have children, or when a loved one dies suddenly, or when a catastrophic accident occurs, when a job is lost - is the loss of an imagined future. That's the profound loss that we grieve but that the world doesn't really have a language for. With loss one has to create a new vision for one's life. One has to reimagine one's life in an entirely new way. It was true for Abraham as he stood on Mount Moriah with his knife raised expecting to sacrifice his son and it has been true for us as we have all had to reimagine our lives this past year.

THERE'S ALWAYS A RAM IN THE THICKET

Abraham never imagined that his story would end with sacrificing a ram anymore than this summers' wedding couples imagined that they would get married in their parents' backyards with 10 people, or spring's *b'nei mitzvah* imagined they would read Torah in their living rooms, or June's graduates imagined they would celebrate from their cars, or fall's new parents imagined they would name their babies online. And yet they all looked up and allowed for new opportunities which in turn led them to finding meaning and hope and a new future.

Abraham's life changes when he does one thing - he looks up and he sees a ram caught in the thicket. The Torah doesn't say that the ram arrived or appeared, rather that it took Abraham just opening his eyes to see it. The Rabbis of the Mishnah imagine that the ram had been there all along. In fact, they say that the ram was created years before in the moments before Shabbat on the last day of creation. (*Avot* 5:5)

We read it today to remind us that there is always a ram in the thicket waiting to be found. I'm not talking about silver linings here. I would not be so crass or simplistic as to suggest that we simply look on the bright side. With 200,000 dead in the United States alone, we're not making lemonade out of our Yom Kippur lemons. Looking and finding the ram in the thicket is rather about persistence in the constant struggle to make meaning in our lives; one of the primary tasks of religious and spiritual existence.

THERE'S ALWAYS A RAM IN THE THICKET

The ram's purpose is to present an alternative to sacrificing Isaac. An alternative that was just waiting there when the expected reality did not come to pass.

We have without a doubt been mired in a thicket. With trees and brush and thorns. And it has been overwhelming and frightening and lonely. But since even before we found ourselves here, there has been a ram just waiting to be discovered.

2020 could be the year of the ram, the spirit animal that represents how we respond and react when our plans fail and our future turns out differently than we hoped and imagined. It appears in the midst of our panic, our disappointment, our fear, and it suggests an alternative, a different way around.

What are the rams in our thickets? What ram might you find? Adult children and grandchildren returned home for long periods of time, more opportunity of exercise and care for our earthly bodies, an opportunity to learn with world class teachers in our own homes, reconnection with long lost friends and college roommates, new relationships with our neighbors, a sharpening of priorities, nurturing our own families from our own kitchens and our own homes, finding out who we are separate from the work that we do.

So many of us come to this Rosh Hashanah so filled with gratitude that we are alive, that we are well, or mostly well, and we are here. And for those who might need a little push towards that sense of gratitude, remember Abraham's advice to look up to the ram.

THERE'S ALWAYS A RAM IN THE THICKET

The poet Yehuda Amichai says that the real hero of the Binding of Isaac was the ram, with his curly wool and his human eyes. (Yehuda Amichai, "The Real Hero") He was the only one in the story who didn't get caught up in what could have been. He was the agent for transformational change. He was the answer to so many questions.

There are years that ask questions and years that answer. Even with the thicket of questions in which we were entangled, this was still a year that answered more than it asked. The answers are all around us, even when we feel tangled up. May we remember to look up and find the ram in the thicket.

Rabbi Debi Wechsler *has been a rabbi at Chizuk Amuno Congregation in Baltimore, Maryland for 22 years.*

THE GOOD ENOUGH SERMON

Rabbi Dr. Raysh Weiss

Every year at this time, we Jews gather to assess our performance – both as a community, and, perhaps even more so, as individuals: How are we doing? Where have we succeeded? Where have we failed? How can we adjust our behavior? How can we do better?

Each year, every one of us faces circumstances that are unique to the particular place and moment in which we find ourselves. Each year comes with its own specific opportunities and its own specific problems, and each year we feel a certain pressure to perform to standards both external and internal, imposed by society and by ourselves. When the High Holidays roll around every year, our self-assessment leads us to consider how we have done in meeting those standards and to resolve to try to make the necessary changes to do better in the coming year. However – as we all know – this year has been unique in its particular set of demands and challenges.

Even more challenging than the pressure to perform is the pressure to perform under pressure. In the last half-year, each of us has found ourselves having to rise to high expectations amidst high stress. For many, the recent months have imposed an unrelenting stream of conflicting demands on us, as we scurry to attend to multiple crises at once. In the thick of a personal and professional ambush, how do we meaningfully compartmentalize and self-preserve?

The more you have invested in routines and solving problems in your life -- the higher-achieving person you are -- the harder this moment is for you. What worked for us previously in our lives cannot be seamlessly applied as a reliable fix right now.

What do we do in the face of an invisible threat that is all too real and impossible to control? What should be our priorities as we are continuously bombarded with an every-expanding list of problems and conflicts that needs addressing? Our brains spin with what seems to be an endless list of things which require our immediate attention. And maybe your old go-getter mindset, which paved the way for your external success, was actually doing a disservice to your inner self all along. And maybe one approach at this moment is to begin to discern between wants and needs and – to borrow from another holiday's liturgy-- to begin to define "dayenu" – to define what is truly "enough."

We live in a high-gloss culture, that places daunting demands on us with regard to our relationships and achievements. We are at once expected to be the perfect professional, the perfect spouse, the perfect parent or the perfect retiree or the perfect child. Worst of all, during in the last couple of decades, with the explosion of social media, we've been socialized to "perform our perfection" outwardly, by constantly projecting to the world an unnaturally sanitized, glistening version of our lives.

Our own obsession with perfection–the external achievement culture we inhabit–all too often becomes a personal trap and a mechanism of our own limitation and self-oppression. Perhaps the unparalleled pressure to achieve in this way explains why Generation Z -- those in the age group from 15 to 21, which is among the most educated generation ever, is reputed to be the most anxious generation yet.

How do we transform the collective and individual anxiety that grips us into something positive? How does our Jewish identity fortify us with a sense of purpose at this moment? I deeply believe that such moments offer us invaluable opportunities to examine who we truly are and where we wish to head – as individuals and as a people. When a crisis hits, it is the time for us to re-evaluate where our true priorities lie. What are our core sustaining values that identify who we are? For what do we stand? And what wisdom can our tradition offer on how we work through this moment?

We can look to examples from Jewish history for some guidance as we seek to adapt and understand what will be enough. Today, I'd like to offer two stories which unearth our core values:

The first is a classic Hasidic tale which tells of how, whenever the Jewish people faced a great threat, the Baal Shem Tov, the great founder of the Hasidic movement, would venture deep into a special place in the forest and meditate. He would light a fire in a special way, recite a prayer, chant a wordless melody or *niggun*, and the crisis would be averted.[29]

---

[29] Introduction to *The Gates of the Forest: A Novel* Elie Wiesel and Frances Frenaye, The Gates Of The Forest. New York: Schocken Books, 1995.

The following generation, when the Jews faced danger, his student, the Maggid of Mezeritch, attempted to do the same thing – he dashed to the forest, identified the spot of his master, and conceded, "Master of the universe – I am unable to light the fire, but I can offer a prayer and a *niggun*." And the Jews were spared.

A generation later, Rabbi Moshe Leib of Sasov, a protegee of the Maggid of Mezeritch, retreated to the very same spot when the Jews were under attack yet again. While Rabbi Moshe Leib knew the spot, he did not know how to light the fire, nor did he know the prayer, nor did he fully know the song. But still, his efforts were enough, and the Jews were saved.

Finally, years later, during the time of Rabbi Yisrael of Rhizin, the Jews yet again faced a perilous situation. Rabbi Yisrael, sitting in his chair at home, threw his face into his hands and cried out to G-d, "Master of the Universe! I know not how to light the special fire, and I unable to recall either the prayer or the song. I can't even locate the place in the forest. But I do remember this story of the Baal Shem Tov. Please have mercy on your people!" and he wept.

And you know what? That was enough. **We don't need to be perfect to be holy**. We don't need to be perfect to be worthy of love and merit a second-chance. In fact, if we *were* perfect, the entire idea of second chances would be irrelevant. We are our stories, and our loved ones and their values live on through our retelling of their stories. Their stories sustain us and become an irreplaceable part of who we are and help us through the most trying times in our lives.

The other story I would like to share with you today on this theme involves the great psychiatrist Viktor Frankl, as he was transferred to Auschwitz during the Holocaust. Viktor Frankl had an entire manuscript written for a book, when he was taken away to the camps and had sewed it into the lining of his coat.[30]

The minute he arrived at Auschwitz, the guards forcibly took his coat away from him. Frankl begged them to spare his coat, but, nevertheless, they ripped it away from him. As was standard practice, the Nazi guards replaced Frankl's fine jacket with a threadbare one taken off the body of a prisoner who had already died in that camp. When Frankl examined the threadbare coat that he had been given, he discovered that its former owner had sewn into the pocket of the coat a single page that contained the verses of the Shema prayer. Frankl understood that as his sign that he was destined to live and that there was a G-d and a greater force with him that would protect him on the very difficult road that lie ahead.

For Frankl, this was the key moment of how he was to understand what was happening to him. How are we to understand what is happening to us?

Our traditional texts have some crucial wisdom to share on this idea. Many know that a traditional mezuzah affixed to the door of a Jewish home contains the text of the *shema*, a reminder of our central credo which so inspired Frankl in the story I just related. But you may

---

[30] Redsand, Anna., 2006. *Viktor Frankl: A Life Worth Living*. New York: Clarion Books, p.70

have wondered about the many mezuzah cases adorned by the Hebrew letter *shin*. Or perhaps you've passed by ones many times without noticing.

Today, I want to focus our attention on the power of this Hebrew letter *shin* and its secret message to us, especially at this time.

We've all been spending much more time in our homes this year. In many of our homes, we have a mezuzah hanging. Many *mezuzot* prominently feature the letter *shin*. Why?

A simple initial explanation is that the *shin* stands for "Shaddai," one of many Hebrew names for G-d. The word "Shaddai" is also traditionally inscribed upon the backs of the mezuzah's parchment.

There is another meaning of Shaddai, though. The Hebrew letters *shin, dalet,* and *yud* stand for *shomer daltot Yisrael,* which means the Guardian of the Doors of Israel. How fitting an image, especially for a time when we stand close to our domestic doors, seeking spiritual guidance and strength.

There is even more behind the Divine image of Shaddai to help us right now. And that is the image of G-d of Enough. In the Talmud (BT Hagiga 12a), we learn that Shaddai also is an acronym for the phrase *"mi sh'amar dai l'olamo"* – that G-d said "Enough" to G-d's world.

THE GOOD ENOUGH SERMON

When G-d created the world, G-d reached a certain point and declared, "Enough!" halting the creation process from reaching its perfect completion.

This particular passage from the Talmud refers to G-d halting the expansion of the sea and the heavens. But G-d also reminds us of what is enough with the seventh day of Creation. Instead of continuing with creation, G-d both mandated and exemplified the Sabbath, Shabbat, a word which is linked in Hebrew to images of sitting and returning. G-d – the Divine Being greater than all Beings in all of time and space -- deemed it urgent and necessary to create a boundary and halt creation. G-d not only created the universe but also introduced the idea of a pause and reflection whose only purpose is to sustain and quietly nourish.

Here we are reminded that G-d intentionally created an imperfect, incomplete world. Indeed, humans, as holy as we may be, are very specifically *not* angels. Angels are merely automatons of G-d's will – literal messengers, devoid of individual agency or free will. What is the meaning of the imperfection G-d sought?

Perhaps our gift as humans is to learn the gift of enough-ness. To *embrace our enough-ness*.

To be very clear – this is *not* a call for mediocrity or a call for apathy; it is to accept and lovingly embrace who we are and allow ourselves to see the beauty both in our potential and in that which we lack.

One of my very favorite teachings, from Vayikra Rabbah, is that a broken vessel is most dear to G-d's

159

heart. It is precisely in our perpetual yearning, our striving, and our acknowledgement of our fragility and enough-ness that we are truly beautiful as humans. Because we know we can be beautiful, even and especially as we embrace our enough-ness, knowing we will never fully master all that there is to know and feel in G-d's spectacular universe.[31]

Powerfully, the Septuagint, the prominent Greek translation of the Bible, renders the Divine name Shaddai as "the sufficient one." As we famously know from our tradition, we were crafted in the image of G-d. What is sufficient about you that you will embrace this year? In what areas do you dream of growing, without torturing yourself with others' expectations of you? Who is the you who is sufficient that will enable you to live and love most meaningfully – who is the you who is sufficient that will paradoxically allow you to grow?

G-d saw to it that we and the very universe we inhabit are inherently incomplete. By creating an incomplete universe, G-d has allowed us to become G-d's partner in the work that is required in order to improve both ourselves and our world.

We are created in the image of G-d. The G-d of *Shaddai* – the G-d that is Sufficient. And you know what? You're doing great.

Maybe you have not snatched the brass rings of our times, whether that is that car you wished to buy, that trip you wished to take, that book you hoped to write,

---

[31] Leviticus Rabbah 7:2

that promotion you hoped to receive, that relationship you had hoped to change, that prize you had hoped to win, or whatever else it might be that would have made for a good, easily likable status update on social media, but you have grown wiser. You have discovered strength you did not know you had. You have acquired new skills. You have increased your awareness. You have persevered. You have given of yourself. You have allowed yourself to take.

Perhaps most importantly, you have discovered your limits, which we now know are holy aspects of your very being. Each one of these internal achievements–the ones you'll never see on Instagram or a Facebook post–are the ones that will carry you through the rest of your life and will allow you to help all of those around you.

You have discovered that you're human. That there's beauty, even and especially in our eternal human imperfections and limitations. We do not operate according to a user's manual. We make mistakes, we learn, and we connect – and *that* is exactly what this season is all about. We are incomplete and need each other. If I felt completely self-sufficient, I would have no call to prayer.

In identifying your limits, you also identify your reserves of strength and energy. that enables you to re-charge right now so that you can be your most intact and rooted "enough" self?

Learning what works is a radical and life-changing act of self-discovery.

THE GOOD ENOUGH SERMON

In his ground-breaking work on attachment theory, 20th century psychoanalyst D.W. Winnicott coined the term "the Good Enough Mother" to describe the process through which a new mother first desperately tries to attend to her infant's every need.

With time, she ultimately sacrifices all of her own basic needs, such as eating and sleeping, in her attempts to comfort her child immediately every time. Eventually, she learns she can pull back just a bit so as to self-preserve. The child may experience a small amount of frustration, but the trade-off is the mother's ability to survive. She thus becomes the Good Enough mother. Which isn't a bad thing! Or to paraphrase a wise man, "you're good enough, you're smart enough, and gosh darnit, people like you." Imagine yourself being sufficient in the image of G-d.

Tonight, the evening of our Kol Nidrei service, I would like to share a powerful idea from my friend and teacher Rabbi Rachel Zerin, who teaches that tonight presents us an opportunity to acknowledge all of the many promises and hopes gone unfulfilled from this last year, as we remember that we already dispensed with those promises and hopes at Kol Nidrei last year. With that in mind, how do we enter into this new year, committing to new dreams and promises while also forgiving ourselves for our own limits?

I'll close with an important line from the musical *Man of No Importance*:

There are glasses to raise in surviving the
day." It is time for us to recognize new
kinds of achievements. Pulling yourself
out of bed. Eating enough. Sleeping
enough. Certainly, affirming someone
else.

To you I say, *l'chayyim*, to life, and to embracing your
enough-ness.

Rabbi Raysh Weiss, *spiritual leader at Congregation Beth
El of Bucks County, PA, holds a Ph.D. from the University of
Minnesota in Comparative Literature and Cultural Studies,
was ordained by the Jewish Theological Seminary, and has
previously served as rabbi of the Shaar Shalom Synagogue in
Halifax, Nova Scotia. Rabbi Weiss is a "good enough" mother
of two and married to Rabbi Jonah Rank. As both a mother of
young children and a rabbi, Rabbi Weiss is often found
saying, "No, we don't eat that!"*

ON CHOOSING LIFE, KINDNESS, AND RESILIENCE

Rabbi Rachel Zerin

What is your primary responsibility?

What is the most important thing for you to give to the rest of the world?

What is it you need most for yourself?

These are the three questions I found myself asking throughout this past year: a year filled with unimaginable challenges and unprecedented situations. A friend of mine recently observed that there is something about a pandemic - or any crisis, for that matter - that urges us to return to the basics. As I have navigated these past several months and all the decisions that I have had to make, particularly as the parent of a five year old, I knew I needed to articulate not only my basic needs, but my basic values, my guiding principles. So I looked at my beautiful child and I asked myself:

What is my greatest responsibility toward you? My greatest goal for you? My greatest hope?

I already partly knew my answer. For years, we have had a saying in our house: "My number 1 job is to keep you healthy and safe." I can't even remember how long ago this became a household mantra, though I do remember where: we were at the pediatrician's office, getting a round of vaccinations, and Ezra was just old enough to look at me with those eyes that say "why are you hurting me? You are supposed to protect me!"

In that instant, the words came to me, crystal clear: my number 1 job is to keep you healthy and safe. Not to keep all bad things from happening to you, because that is impossible. Not to protect you from all pain, because sometimes pain is necessary in the short term. But to keep you healthy and safe.

Ever since, it has remained a household mantra, and it has seen us through many a difficult time: it has seen undesired vegetables get eaten; hands get washed with that dreaded thing called soap; teeth get brushed with toothpaste even though it tastes yucky, and more.

This year, however, I realized that this was not enough. Don't get me wrong -- health and safety remain my most important responsibility. But the past year has presented me with situations that required additional guideposts, either because health and safety were a given, and I had to make decisions based on other values at play; or because health and safety would be at risk no matter what I did, and so I needed to clarify which other values would serve as guideposts as I navigated this complicated world in which we live.

After a long process of introspection and reflection, a lot of prayer, and a lot conversations with friends, mentors, and my therapist, my one-line saying became a three-fold mantra, each line answering one of those questions:

ON CHOOSING LIFE, KINDNESS, AND RESILIENCE

My number 1 job is to keep you healthy and safe.

My number 1 goal is that you be kind.

My number 1 hope is that you be resilient.

These three things have been my guiding principles in this turbulent time. I quickly realized that they were not only my hopes and goals for Ezra, they were also my hopes and goals for myself - because, as is so often the case, it is far easier to articulate the things we want for the people we love the most than it is for ourselves. In every decision I had to make, these values have steered me to the right path. Whenever I feel unsure, I ask myself "does this accomplish my job of keeping us healthy and safe? Does this further my goal that you be kind? Does this help you be resilient?". If the answer is no, I recalibrate; if the answer is yes, I move forward. These three things have become my guiding lights; through unimaginable decisions and unprecedented challenges, they have not failed me yet.

When I thought about what message I wanted to share with you today, I kept coming back to this one. Because I realized that these are not just my guiding values for my child, or myself; this is also my prayer for the world, for each and every one of you.

And while I came to articulate these values - of health and safety, of kindness, of resilience - through my own process of introspection, I know these values are also deeply embedded in our Jewish tradition.

ON CHOOSING LIFE, KINDNESS, AND RESILIENCE

And so, on this Rosh Hashanah Day, as we begin 5781, I want to offer this prayer for the world; this prayer for each and every one of us:

May we always choose life

May we live lives of kindness

May we be blessed with resilience

Choosing life is the foundation. Without basic health and safety, we cannot do much else. Jewish tradition recognizes this in saying that *pikuach nefesh*, the preservation of life, takes precedence over nearly every other mitzvah in our tradition. Jewish law clearly instructs us to protect our own lives, even at the cost of other mitzvot; and it instructs us to not stand idly by while our neighbors' lives are at stake, even if intervening to save their lives comes at a cost to ourselves.

I don't have to convince you that protecting our health and safety is harder this year than perhaps ever before. In part, the greatest challenge is not in preserving our own life so much as in preserving the health and safety of others. Now more than ever, keeping each other healthy and safe demands of us a radical selflessness, which we are not programmed for. It means making ourselves uncomfortable. It means making sacrifices, missing out on experiences we wish we could have. But this is what Judaism demands of us. And so this year I pray: may our number 1 job be to keep each other healthy and safe. May we always choose life.

ON CHOOSING LIFE, KINDNESS, AND RESILIENCE

While they are a necessary foundation, health and safety are not enough. When I think about who I want Ezra to be, what I want him to put out into the world - and what I want myself, and all of us, to put out into the world - the answer is clear: kindness. Of all the interpersonal mitzvot, of all the attributes we are asked to cultivate, kindness, *hesed*, seems to me to be the most important.

One could argue that the Torah itself labels kindness as the prime attribute, the most important way of interacting with others. In Massechet Sotah, from the Talmud, Rabbi Simlai says:

תורה תחלתה גמילות חסדים וסופה
גמילות חסדים

> The Torah begins with acts of lovingkindness, and it ends with acts of lovingkindness.

> It begins with acts of loving kindness, as it is written: "God made for Adam and his wife garments of skin, and clothed them."

> And it ends with acts of loving kindness, as it is written: "and God buried Moses in the valley".

What Rabbi Simlai is pointing out is that the Torah is bookended with kindness. God's first interaction with human beings is an act of lovingkindness: Adam and Eve are naked, and are ashamed, and God clothes them; and the last interaction recorded in the Torah between God and human beings is an act of lovingkindness:

ON CHOOSING LIFE, KINDNESS, AND RESILIENCE

Moses dies, and God, God's self, buries him. Implicit in this is not only that kindness is the most important attribute, but perhaps also that the Torah is essentially a book about kindness. If you had to summarize the Torah in one phrase, Rabbi Simlai might simply say exactly what the author Neil Gaiman wrote in his children's book "Blueberry Girl" thousands of years later: "First, may you always be Kind."

My prayer is not only about your greatest responsibility, or the most important thing you give to the world. It is also my greatest hope. As this unbelievably difficult year has unfolded, one thing became clear. My greatest hope is not that you have a perfect life or be protected from all bad things, because that is impossible. My greatest hope is that you have the tools to face the challenges that come your way; the inner strength to weather the storms. My number one hope is that you are resilient.

Resilience in Judaism is a funny thing. When it comes to the Jewish people, one could claim there is no greater defining characteristic than our resilience. We are the people who survive, who rebound, who persevere no matter how great the threat or how dire the circumstances. Think of our holidays. Passover, Purim, Hanukkah - they tried to destroy us, but we survived. We are resilient! This is not even to mention numerous times throughout history when our people have been oppressed, or exiled, or forced to abandon Judaism, and yet, we have continued to survive. Time after time, our people have proved resilient.

ON CHOOSING LIFE, KINDNESS,
AND RESILIENCE

When it comes to individual resilience, the examples from Jewish tradition are not quite so readily available - probably because resilience as a term, a coherent concept, is very modern, and so we do not find "resilience" as a single term used in the Bible or by the rabbis. There are, however, many Jewish texts, and concepts, and traditions that speak to the various characteristics of resilience. I want to share one such story with you now.

You may have heard me share this story from the Talmud earlier this year, but hopefully like me, you will learn a little bit more from this story every time you hear it.

It's a story about Rabban Gamliel, who was once journeying on a ship; and his friend and colleague, the great Rabbi Akiva, was journeying alongside him, on another ship. During their journey, a terrible storm came, and Rabban Gamliel watched while Rabbi Akiva's ship sank. Gamliel mourned for the loss of his friend, and the loss of the Torah that the entire world would be without because Rabbi Akiva was not in it. But when Rabban Gamliel disembarked from his journey, he couldn't believe his eyes, because who was sitting on the shore? Rabbi Akiva, there, teaching Torah.

> Gamliel asked Akiva: *"B'ni,* My son, who brought you up from the water?"
>
> Akiva replied: *daf shel s'finah nizdamen li,* a plank of wood came to me, *v'khol gal vagal she-ba alai, ne-enanti li roshi.* And when each

and every wave came upon me, I bowed
my head before it, swam into it, let it crash
over me, and in that way I returned to
the shore.

The events of this past year have often felt like a terrible
storm, with wave after wave crashing over us.
Pandemic. Loss of physical community. Illness, and
death. Continuing reminders of the racial injustice in
our country. Fires burning our beautiful west coast to
the ground. Not to mention the personal struggles so
many of us have faced. Navigating this year has felt like
being lost at sea, storm-tossed, with only a plank to hold
onto. But this story is a reminder that one need not be
lost, just because of the storm. That the waves crashing
over us need not drown us. I see this not only as a story
of survival, but a story that can teach us three key
lessons for building our own resilience.

The first is that resilience requires us to accept our
situation and face our challenges head on, neither
ignoring them nor catastrophizing them. This seems so
counterintuitive, and yet, time and time again I have
found this to be true. Think about Rabbi Akiva. When
his ship sank, he could have tried to ignore the problem
- but pretending to be in a ship when there wasn't one
wouldn't have ended well; or, he could have
acknowledged the loss of his ship and jumped to the
conclusion that all was lost, as Rabban Gamliel did -
which also would have changed the ending of the story,
and not for good. Once at sea, you might have expected
him to swim away from each wave that came toward
him, but he didn't. Instead, he faced each wave and

allowed it to go over him. He recognized the loss of his ship, he accepted his situation, and he faced his challenges, literally head on. Because of that, the Talmud says, he was able to make it back, safely, to shore.

Perhaps this approach would help us build our personal resilience, too. This year has been filled with so many challenging circumstances. But have we accepted these circumstances? Have we tried to avoid them, hoping they will just go away? Or have we catastrophized and gone directly to playing the worst case scenario game? I can tell you that I have done all of these, at various times. But it is the times when I have paused, taken a realistic assessment of my circumstances, and accepted things for what they are that I have been most able to adapt and feel a sense of strength and calm.

Rabbi Akiva's acceptance of his situation leads directly to the second lesson this story offers: the importance of adaptability. Again, we see this in the contrast between Rabban Gamliel and Rabbi Akiva. Rabban Gamliel saw Akiva's ship sink, and assumed that without the ship, Akiva had no other means to make it to shore. Akiva, on the other hand, lost his ship and immediately adapted. He knew he couldn't control his circumstances, so instead he controlled his response, grabbing on to the next thing he could find that would keep him afloat: the plank, which brought him safely to dry land.

Not only was Akiva as an individual adaptable; the story of the Jewish people is filled with examples of adaptability. The very fact that we are here in synagogue, praying on Rosh Hashanah is an example of our adaptability. This holiday was originally celebrated by bringing sacrifices to the Temple, but when the Temple was destroyed, our people adapted. Rather than abandoning Judaism, they created a new worship system, one whose basic structure continues to this day. Knowing how adaptable our people has been gives me strength. If our ancestors could adapt and survive such a giant shift, then perhaps we can adapt to our current situation, too.

The final lesson this story of Rabbi Akiva teaches us is the importance of connectedness in cultivating resilience: connectedness to community and connectedness to God. On a first read, this lesson is not at all apparent. However, there is an interesting feature of the Hebrew in this text. There are many words in rabbinic Hebrew that could refer to a ship's plank. The word chosen here is *daf*, a word that can mean both "plank," or "column of written text" - particularly, a column of rabbinic text. You may be familiar with this word - nowadays, we use the word "daf" to refer to a page of Talmud, as in "daf yomi". If we read this story through an interpretive lens, we read, then, a story of a rabbi, alone at sea, not certain of his survival, reaching out and grabbing onto a *daf*, that is, a page of sacred teachings, perhaps written by his colleagues and friends. In what could easily have been the loneliest moment, Akiva finds connection to his community, and connection to God.

Connectedness is one of the most important components of resilience. And Judaism offers us so many blessings of connection. We are connected to our Temple Emanu-El community - even, when we cannot physically gather in the same room. We are connected to our people - to thousands of years of tradition, to generations of ancestors who came before us. We utter the same prayers, we study the same texts, we observe the same sacred traditions - and even if we have our own special way of doing all these things, when we do them, we are never alone, because we are connected to countless others who have done them before, or who are engaged in these practices right now, across the span of the globe.

And most importantly, we are connected to the Holy Blessed One.

I have always been moved by the idea that we are all created in the image of God, and that every person contains within themselves the spark of the Divine. This idea traces back to the very beginning of the Torah, when humanity was created. I have long wondered what the world would be like if we truly treated each other as if we were interacting with a refraction of the Divine.

This year, I came to realize - obvious though it should be - that if each and person contains within us the spark of the Divine, that means that I, too, have that spark. That this should not only impact the way we treat others, it should also impact the way we perceive ourselves. If I contain within myself a spark of the Divine, then no matter where I am, or what is happening, or how alone I may feel, I am still always connected to God.

This year, I began a practice of placing my hand on my heart and taking a deep breath whenever I start to feel overwhelmed - similar to our new concluding ritual at the end of services. I learned this at a workshop I participated in on mindful self-compassion this past January. Breath is such a powerful image in Judaism. Of course, breath is what sustains us. But breath - and specifically, God's breath - is what originally gave us life. The second chapter of B'reishit tells us that the first human being was not animated until God breathed the breath of life into him.

Over the course of these past several months, I began to wonder, if the first human being was created with Divine breath, and I am a descendant of that human being, do I have that Divine Breath in me, too? And if I place my hand on my heart, and breathe deeply enough, might it be possible to breathe past the well of my own breath, and to access some of that Divine Breath, that Divine Spark that is in all of us? This connection has been a well of resilience for me. Maybe it can be a well of resilience for all of us.

My number one job is to keep you healthy and safe

My number one goal is that you be kind

My number one hope is that you be resilient

ON CHOOSING LIFE, KINDNESS, AND RESILIENCE

I first wrote this prayer as a parent. But the more I thought about it, the more I wondered if this might perhaps also be the prayer of The Parent. So now, I ask: *Avinu Malkeinu*, our Parent, our Sovereign, *Melekh Hafetz Bahayyim*, Ruler who Desires Life, is it your prayer, too, that we always choose life? *Rachamana*, Merciful One, whose first interaction with humanity was kindness and whose last interaction with humanity in the Torah was kindness, is it your foremost goal, too, that we be kind? *Elohim she-nafach bi nishmat hayyim*, God, who breathed into me the breath of life, is your greatest hope that we realize our resilience?

I want to invite you to take your hand, and place it on your heart. Close your eyes, if you'd like. Feel your heart beat in your chest. Think of the kindness you want to show to the world. Take a deep breath, and try to feel all the ways that our breath connects us: to our selves, to others, and to God.

A Rosh Hashanah prayer for my child. A prayer for myself. A prayer for the world. And perhaps, God's prayer for us, too.

As we enter 5781:

May we always choose life

May we live lives of kindness

May we be blessed with resilience

Amen.

176

ON CHOOSING LIFE, KINDNESS, AND RESILIENCE

Rabbi Rachel Zerin *currently serves as the assistant rabbi at Temple Emanu-El in Providence, RI. She was ordained from the Jewish Theological Seminary in 2015, where she also received her MA in Talmud. While at JTS, Rabbi Zerin served as student rabbi of Temple B'nai Shalom of Benton Harbor, MI and the Flemington Jewish Community Center in NJ, and intern at Rutgers Hillel. Rabbi Zerin's interests include Talmud, innovative ritual, social justice, and interfaith dialogue. Prior to her rabbinical studies, Rabbi Zerin studied at the Conservative Yeshiva in Jerusalem, and earned her BA in Voice Performance and Religion from Syracuse University.*

Printed in Great Britain
by Amazon

83945985R00112